Leckie×Leckie

Scotland's leading educational publishers

National 5
HEALTH & FOOD TECHNOLOGY
SUCCESS GUIDE

N5 HEALTH & FOOD TECHNOLOGY SUCCESS GUIDE

Katrina Cameron • Karen Coull
Gail Reid

© 2013 Leckie & Leckie Ltd
Cover image © K. Miri Photography

001/29072013

10 9 8 7 6 5 4 3 2 1

ISBN 9780007504824

Published by
Leckie & Leckie Ltd
An imprint of HarperCollins*Publishers*
Westerhill Road, Bishopbriggs, Glasgow, G64 2QT
T: 0844 576 8126   F: 0844 576 8131
leckieandleckie@harpercollins.co.uk   www.leckieandleckie.co.uk

Special thanks to
Donna Cole (copy-edit); Q2A Bill Smith (layout); Ink Tank (cover design); Joanna Chisholm (proofread); Jill Laidlaw (proofread)

Printed in Italy by Lego, S.P.A.

A CIP Catalogue record for this book is available from the British Library.

Acknowledgements
We would like to thank the following for permission to reproduce photographs. Page numbers are followed, where necessary, by t (top), b (bottom), m (middle), l (left) or r (right).

P8 iStockphoto, p9 iStockphoto, p10l iStockphoto, p10r iStockphoto, p11l iStockphoto, p11m Gyuszko-Photo, p11r Evgenia Sh, p12l Ingram Publishing, p12r Sandra Caldwell, p13l iStockphoto, p13m iStockphoto, p13r iStockphoto, p14 Tischenko Irina, 15t Dulce Rubia, 15m Elenamiv, 15b iStockphoto, p16l Tischenko Irina, p16tr Robyn Mackenzie, p16br Robyn Mackenzie, p17 Aaron Amat, p18 Tish1, p19 Robyn Mackenzie,

p20t iStockphoto, p20b iStockphoto, p21 iStockphoto, p22t iStockphoto, p22b Jupiterimages, p23t iStockphoto, p23b Jupiterimages, p24t YanLev, p24b iStockphoto, p25 iStockphoto, p26t iStockphoto, p26b Alila Medical Images, p27b Hemera, p29t tacar, p29m Scisetti Alfio , p29b iStockphoto, p30t Africa Studio, p30b Picsfive, p32t iStockphoto, p32b Juriah Mosin, p33t Diedie, p33m Lisa F. Young, p33b iStockphoto, p34 Rafal Olechowski, p35 Anatoliy Samara, p36 Image Source, p37 Indigo Fish, p38 Voronin76, p39 Martin Novak, p40 iStockphoto, p43t foodonwhite, p43b Eskemar, p44 iStockphoto, p45l iStockphoto, p45r iStockphoto, p47 iStockphoto, p48 Food & Drug Administration/Science Photo Library, p50l iStockphoto, p50r iStockphoto, p54t iStockphoto, p54l Evikka, p54m karamysh, p54r bitt24, p55 Jiri Hera , p56t Africa Studio, p56l Marie C Fields, p56m ffolas, p57l Warren Price Photography, p57m bergamont, p57r Mike Flippo, p58b Dorling Kindersley, p59l WimL, p59b Brent Hofacker, p60t iStockphoto. p60m iStockphoto, p60b iStockphoto, p62t Noel Hendrickson, p62m Digital Vision, p62b iStockphoto, p64 Joe Gough/Nayashkova Olga, p65t iStockphoto, p67 Franck Boston, p68 Kharkhan Oleg, p69tl Stockbyte, p69tr koko-tewan, p69bl tukkata, p69br Kharkhan Oleg, p70t Getty Images, p72 africa924, p73 Peter Bernik, p74t Peter Bernik, p74b Alison Hancock, p145b iStockphoto, p76bl Elovich, p76bm iStockphoto, p76br iStockphoto, p78t iStockphoto, p78b Stockbyte, p80l iStockphoto, p80t iStockphoto, p80r iStockphoto, p80b T.W. van Urk, p82 iStockphoto, p83t iStockphoto, p83m Joe Gough, p83b Anna Sedneva, p86 Yeko Photo Studio, p88 iStockphoto, p90 Jaimie Duplass, p91l Brian A Jackson, p91r iStockphoto, p92 Brian A Jackson, P96t Art Allianz, p98t iStockphoto, p98m Brian A Jackson, p98b iStockphoto

We would like to thank the following organisations for permission to reproduce logos.

P65 Vegetarian Society, p70 Soil Association, p80 Fairtrade, p87 Benecol, p92 Food Standards Agency, p93 Trading Standards Institute, p92 Citizens Advice, p95 *Which?* (The copyright in this material is owned by *Which?* Limited and has been reproduced here with their permission. The material and logo must not be reproduced in whole or in part without the written permission of *Which?* Limited)

Contents

Unit 1 – Food for health

Unit 2: Food product development

Unit 3: Contemporary food issues

National 5 Health and Food Technology

National 5 Health & Food Technology is a practical-based course that consists of three units, an assignment and an exam.

The Units

Food for health	Food product development	Contemporary food issues
When you have completed this unit, you should be able to: 1. Explain the relationship between health, food and nutrition 2. Demonstrate knowledge and understanding of dietary needs, for individuals at various stages of life 3. Explain current dietary advice 4. Through practical activities, make and reflect on food products which meet individual needs.	When you have completed this unit, you should be able to: 1. Demonstrate knowledge and understanding of the functional properties of ingredients in food and their uses in developing new food products 2. Demonstrate an understanding of the stages involved in developing food products 3. Through a problem solving approach, develop food products to meet specified needs 4. Apply knowledge and understanding of safe and hygienic food practices.	When you have completed this unit, you should be able to: 1. Demonstrate knowledge and understanding of consumer food choice 2. Explain factors which may affect food choices and contemporary food issues 3. Describe technological developments in food and organisations which protect consumers' interests 4. Demonstrate knowledge and understanding of food labelling and how it helps consumers make informed choices 5. Apply knowledge and skills in practical contexts.

SQA 2013

Course Assessment

Unit Assessment

You will work through all three units in school and your practical skills will be assessed throughout these units. Each unit may be assessed independently, or your school may decide to combine assessments so that they cover two or all three of the units.

You may be asked to complete tasks independently to demonstrate your understanding of the course content. This could be done in a number of different ways, including completing a project, test, presentation, poster or developing a new product.

Unit assessments must be passed for you to complete the course. However, they do not contribute to your overall grade.

Course Assessment

The course assessment will assess your ability to integrate and apply knowledge from across all three units.

Assignment

The assignment is worth 50% of the total marks for the course assessment (completed in school).

You will complete a food product development task in response to a brief provided by SQA. The assignment will involve you planning and producing an idea for a food product, then testing and evaluating the suitability of your product against the original brief. This will be completed independently in school and will be sent to SQA to be marked.

Question paper

The question paper is worth 50% of the total marks for the course assessment.

The exam lasts for 1 hour 30 minutes. The question paper will consist of five questions, each worth ten marks. See pages 100–104 in this book for more information and guidance on the course question paper.

TOP TIP

Use the Glossary on pages 105–107 to look up any words you don't understand from each of the three units.

Benefits to health of a balanced and varied diet

What is a balanced diet?

A **diet** is what all individuals eat or drink on a daily basis.

A **balanced diet** is when a person eats a **variety** of foods and drinks that will provide them with the correct amount of nutrients their body needs.

Food

- Individuals need to make choices about which **foods** they should eat and drink each day for all their meals and snacks.
- Choosing foods from each of the food groups can help individuals eat a **varied diet**.
- All foods can contribute to a balanced diet if they are eaten in the correct proportions.

Nutrition

- The **nutrients** protein, fat, carbohydrate, vitamins and minerals are found in food.
- All foods contain at least one **nutrient** that has a specific job to do in the body.
- Water and dietary fibre are also needed by the body.
- Different people need different quantities of **nutrients** depending on their:
    - activity levels
    - age
    - gender (male or female)
    - height (tall or short)
    - health.

Health

Getting the balance wrong in a diet by eating too much or too little of food and drink can contribute to diet-related diseases.

Too much of this	Can lead to this
Fat	• obesity • coronary heart disease
Salt	• high blood pressure • coronary heart disease
Sugar	• dental caries (tooth decay) • obesity • Type 2 diabetes

Too little of this	Can lead to this
Fruit and vegetables	• cancers • coronary heart disease • colds and flu
Oily fish	• coronary heart disease • strokes
Water Dietary fibre	• constipation • bowel disorders

Health benefits of a balanced diet

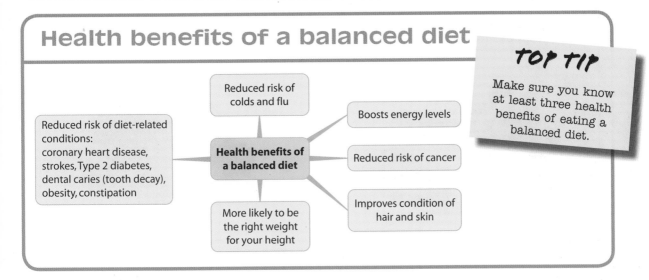

TOP TIP

Make sure you know at least three health benefits of eating a balanced diet.

Quick Test

Read statements 1–4. Some are facts about **balanced diets** and some are fibs! For each fib, change the statement so it becomes a fact.

Statement	Change needed to make the statement correct
Eating less fat will reduce the risk of tooth decay.	
Eating less salt will reduce the risk of high blood pressure.	
Eating more fruit and vegetables will prevent colds and flu.	
Eating more oily fish will prevent Type 2 diabetes.	

Macronutrients 1: protein and carbohydrate

It is important for good health to eat a **balanced diet**. A balanced diet provides all the necessary **nutrients** in the correct proportions and quantities to meet our needs. One way to follow a balanced diet is to make sure we eat a variety of foods that supply a range of nutrients. **Macronutrients** are the main components of our diet and are therefore needed in larger quantities. The three **macronutrients** are **protein, fat and carbohydrates** – all of these perform essential roles in the human body.

Protein	
Function of nutrient	For growth, repair and maintenance of body tissues. **Excess protein can be used as a secondary source of energy.**
Characteristics	Protein is made up of building blocks called amino acids. **High biological value** (HBV) protein contains all eight essential amino acids. **Low biological value** (LBV) protein lacks one or more essential amino acids.
Food sources	HBV – mainly animal sources (meat, fish, eggs, milk). LBV – mainly plant sources (beans, lentils, nuts). High biological value protein Low biological value protein
Effect on health	Too much of the nutrient: excess protein is broken down and used as a source of energy. This energy can lead to weight gain if it is not expended.

Carbohydrate

Function of nutrient	Provides the body with **energy** for all activities.
	Aids digestion by supplying dietary fibre (sometimes known as non starch polysaccharide, NSP) to the body.

Characteristics

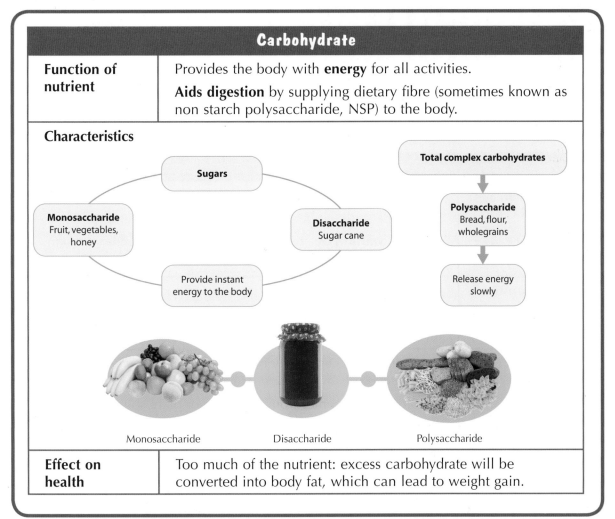

Monosaccharide	Disaccharide	Polysaccharide

Effect on health	Too much of the nutrient: excess carbohydrate will be converted into body fat, which can lead to weight gain.

Quick Test

1. Give the difference between HBV protein and LBV protein.
2. Give an example of an HBV and LBV protein.
3. Which type of carbohydrate provides the body with a slow release of energy?
4. What can happen to the body if too much protein and carbohydrate are eaten?

Macronutrients 2: fats–saturated fat and unsaturated fat

Fat	
Function of nutrient	Provides a concentrated source of energy. Provides a source of fat–soluble vitamins A, D, E and K. Provides **warmth** by creating an insulating layer under the skin. Protects vital organs.
Characteristics	Fat can either be 'visible' or 'invisible' in foods. Visible fat = the white fat on the edge of bacon. Invisible fat = the fat in cakes.
Food sources	Saturated fat comes mainly from animal sources: meat, butter, cheese. Unsaturated fat comes from vegetable or plant sources: avocado, olive oil.

Saturated fat   Unsaturated fat

Effect on health	Too much of the nutrient: too much saturated fat can lead to weight gain and/or obesity.

Saturated fat	
Function of nutrient	Eat in moderation as a diet high in saturated fats can increase bad cholesterol, which in turn can lead to heart disease.
Characteristics	Normally a solid at room temperature. **Health tips**: Remove all visible saturated fat before cooking. Grill meat to allow fat to drip away.
Food Sources	Found mainly in animal sources: butter, cream, meat, cheese.

Unsaturated fat	
Function of nutrient	**Polyunsaturated fats**: help to bring down cholesterol levels in the body. **Monounsaturated fats**: help to reduce the bad cholesterol caused by saturated fats. **Essential fatty acids**: omega-3 helps to reduce the risk of a blood clot forming, thereby preventing heart disease.
Characteristics	Normally liquid at room temperature.
Food sources	**Polyunsaturated fats**: sunflower oil, nuts. **Monounsaturated fats**: olive oil, avocado. **Essential fatty acids**: oily fish like mackerel or salmon. Polyunsaturated fats Monounsaturated fats Essential fatty acids

Quick Test

1. Explain why you should limit the amount of saturated fat in your diet.
2. Identify a food source of omega-3 and explain its positive effect on health.
3. Look at the pizza recipe below. Choose two foods and identify the macronutrients in each. State two functions in the body for each of these nutrients.

Ham and pineapple pizza	
For the dough	**For the topping**
400g strong white flour	2 tbsp chopped tomatoes
2 tsp salt	10ml tomato purée
15g fresh yeast	4 slices ham
275ml water	25g pineapple
50ml olive oil	50g grated cheese

Micronutrients 1: vitamins

Micronutrients are commonly referred to as **vitamins and minerals**. They are called 'micro' as the body only needs very small quantities of them. Nevertheless, they are essential for good health and deficiencies can lead to serious dietary diseases.

Vitamins

Water-soluble vitamins vitamin B and C	
General characteristics	Water-soluble vitamins cannot be stored in the body so they need to be consumed daily. Water-soluble vitamins are easily lost or destroyed during storage, preparation and cooking.
Characteristics of vitamin B group	The **vitamin B group release energy from food**: **Vitamin B1** – releases energy from carbohydrate and helps the nervous system function (milk, meat, bread). **Vitamin B2** – releases energy from proteins, carbohydrates and fats; essential for growth in children (milk, meat, green vegetables). **Folic acid** – helps form red blood cells; protects against neural tube defect (spina bifida) in unborn babies (green leafy vegetables, liver, fortified breakfast cereals).
Characteristics of vitamin C	**Vitamin C** helps fight infections, heals wounds quicker and forms connective tissues in the body. It is also an antioxidant, which helps reduce the risk of heart disease and some cancers. Sources of vitamin C are: oranges, strawberries, potatoes, green vegetables.

TOP TIP

Try to eat more vegetables than fruits as they have a lower sugar content.

Fat-soluble vitamins vitamin A, vitamin D and vitamin E	
General characteristics	Fat-soluble vitamins are stored in the body so they do not need to be consumed daily.
Characteristics of vitamin A	Vitamin A is required for growth in children and is necessary for good eyesight, especially in dim light. It is also an antioxidant, which helps reduce the risk of heart disease and some cancers. Vitamin A is found in liver, carrots and margarine. 
Effect on health	A lack of vitamin A can lead to poor night vision.
Characteristics of vitamin D	Vitamin D helps absorb calcium. It works together with phosphorous to develop strong bones and teeth and prevents rickets in children. Vitamin D is found in sunlight, oily fish, egg yolk and fortified breakfast cereals. Vitamin D is in an interrelationship with calcium and phosphorous.
Effect on health	A lack of vitamin D can lead to rickets.
Characteristics of vitamin E	Vitamin E maintains cell membranes. It is also an antioxidant, which helps reduce the risk of heart disease and some cancers. Vitamin E is found in vegetable oil, green leafy vegetables and peanuts.

Quick Test

Identify if the statements below are facts or fibs. For every answer that is a fib, change the statement so it becomes a fact.

Statement	Change needed to make the statement correct
Water-soluble vitamins are stored in the body.	
Vitamin B1 releases energy from carbohydrate.	
Vitamin C is an antioxidant vitamin.	
Folic acid helps to form white blood cells.	
Vitamins A, D, E are fat soluble.	
Vitamin A is found in carrots.	
You get vitamin D when you are exposed to the dark.	
Vitamin D absorbs iron.	

Micronutrients 2: minerals

Minerals

Iron

Function of the nutrient	Needed to form red blood cells in the body (haemoglobin). Red blood cells transport oxygen around the body.
Characteristics of iron	Iron is in an interrelationship with vitamin C. Iron is needed in the body to help to prevent anaemia.
Sources of iron	Red meat, green leafy vegetables, fortified breakfast cereals and breads.

Effect on health	Lack of iron can lead to anaemia.

Calcium

Function of the nutrient	Required for the growth and development of bones and teeth. Helps in the normal clotting of blood. For normal functioning of muscles and nerves.
Characteristics of calcium	Calcium is in an interrelationship with phosphorous and vitamin D.
Effect on health	Calcium is needed in the body to help prevent osteoporosis and rickets. Lack of calcium can lead to osteoporosis.
Sources of calcium	Milk, cheese, yoghurt, flour, dried fruits, nuts and tinned fish with bones.

Sodium	
Function of the nutrient	Essential for maintaining correct water balance in the body. Required for correct muscle and nerve activity. For normal functioning of muscles and nerves.
Spot the difference	Salt contains both sodium and chloride. It is the sodium in salt that can be bad for our health. Sodium is one contributing factor to high blood pressure.
Sources of sodium	Table salt, canned foods, savoury snacks and bacon.
Effect on health	Too much sodium can lead to high blood pressure.

Quick Test

Identify if each statement below is a fact or a fib. For every answer that is a fib, change the statement so it becomes a fact.

Statement	Change needed to make the statement correct
Lack of iron in the body can cause anaemia.	
Red meat is high in iron.	
Calcium makes bones weak.	
Calcium is found in milk, cheese and yoghurt.	
Salt consists of sodium and phosphorous.	
Salt helps to maintain water balance in the body.	

Water and dietary fibre

As well as macro- and micro-nutrients, the other two components essential for a balanced diet are water and dietary fibre (NSP).

Water

Functions

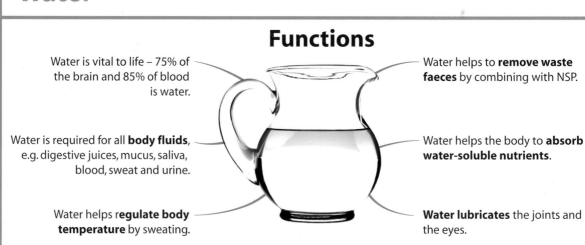

Water is vital to life – 75% of the brain and 85% of blood is water.

Water helps to **remove waste faeces** by combining with NSP.

Water is required for all **body fluids**, e.g. digestive juices, mucus, saliva, blood, sweat and urine.

Water helps the body to **absorb water-soluble nutrients**.

Water helps r**egulate body temperature** by sweating.

Water lubricates the joints and the eyes.

Sources of water:
- tap water
- fruit and vegetables
- all drinks – juices, milk, tea and coffee.

Dietary fibre

- **Soluble fibre** dissolves in water and acts like a **sponge** to moderate blood sugar levels and remove cholesterol.
- It gives the **feeling of fullness**.
- **Insoluble fibre** does not dissolve in water and acts like a broom to sweep out the digestive tract.
- It makes faeces soft and bulky helping to prevent constipation and bowel disorders.

Sources of fibre

Soluble fibre	Insoluble fibre
Oats	Whole grains
Beans	Fruit with skin on
Fruit and vegetables	Vegetables

TOP TIP

Make sure you drink at least eight glasses of water a day and have a high-fibre diet, as these work together to help prevent constipation and bowel diseases.

Quick Test

1. State two functions of water.
2. Give one example of a soluble fibre and explain what it does in the body.
3. Give one example of an insoluble fibre and explain what it does in the body.
4. Explain why you should have enough water and dietary fibre in your diet.

Interrelationships of nutrients

Most foods contain more than one nutrient, but hardly any food contains them all. By combining certain foods we can heighten the effect of nutrients. Look at the three interrelationships below.

Calcium, phosphorous and vitamin D

Interrelationship	Calcium + phosphorous + vitamin D = strong bones and teeth.
Food sources	Calcium: milk, cheese. Phosphorous: milk, fish. Vitamin D: sunshine, oily fish.
How they work together	Vitamin D assists the absorption of calcium in the body. Without it the body cannot use the calcium in food. Calcium and phosphorous join together to create 'calcium phosphate', which helps to form and give strength to bones and teeth enamel.
Food that hinder absorption	Too much fibre (NSP) in the diet can hinder absorption. A diet high in fat. Phytic acid.
Example meal	Egg sandwich and a glass of milk.

Iron and vitamin C

Interrelationship	Iron + vitamin C prevents anaemia.
Food sources	Iron: red meat, breakfast cereals. Vitamin C: potatoes, oranges.
How they work together	Vitamin C is needed to change iron into a form that the body can easily absorb, i.e. from ferric iron to ferrous iron.
Food that hinders absorption	Too much fibre (NSP) in the diet can hinder absorption. Phytic acid.
Example meal	Breakfast cereal and orange juice.

The ACE vitamins

Interrelationship	Vitamins A, C and E – the ACE vitamins – reduce the risk of heart disease and some cancers.
Food sources	Vitamin A: carrots, liver. Vitamin C: oranges, peppers. Vitamin E: eggs, margarine.
How they work together	The ACE vitamins are most commonly known as antioxidants. They help to neutralise potentially damaging free radicals in the body. Vitamin E improves the activity of vitamin A in the body. Once vitamin E has been used in the body, vitamin C helps to recycle it, therefore enhancing its action.
Example meal	Carrot and orange soup and a slice of bread with margarine.

TOP TIP

Eat a balanced varied diet as no single food provides the body with all the nutrients that it requires to function properly.

Quick Test

Look at the menu below. For each part of the menu identify:

1. the nutrients
2. whether any interrelationship is present
3. any factors that could hinder absorption.

Starter

Chicken liver pâté with toasted brioche and sticky orange marmalade

Main

Vegetable quiche (peppers, courgettes, carrots and mushrooms)

Dessert

Strawberry cheesecake (biscuit base)

Dietary diseases: obesity and heart disease

Obesity

Diet-related causes
- diets high in fats and sugars
- eating more calories than are expended
- diet low in total complex carbohydrates
- diet low in fruit and vegetables

Lifestyle-related causes
- lack of exercise

Effect on health

Obesity is a hazard to health because of the **excess body fat** created by **long-term overeating**.

Obesity can lead to a number of other health problems:
- strain on the heart increases the risk of **heart disease**
- a greater risk of **high blood pressure**.

Dietary prevention
- have a diet high in ACE vitamins and total complex carbohydrates
- reduce non-milk extrinsic (NME) sugar intake
- reduce fat intake
- reduce portion size

Lifestyle prevention
- Be more physically active – this will reduce stress and help to reduce body weight. Our energy intake must be lower than our energy expenditure to use up the excess fat.
- Reduce alcohol intake.

Heart disease

Diet-related causes
- being overweight
- diet high in saturated fat
- high blood pressure
- diet high in salt

Lifestyle-related causes
- stress
- insufficient exercise
- smoking
- high alcohol intake

Other causes
- hereditary factors
- increasing age
- gender: men are more likely to suffer from heart disease than women

A build-up of cholesterol gradually narrows the arteries.

Effect on health

A diet high in saturated fat can lead to a build-up of **cholesterol** (fatty deposits) which will gradually **narrow the arteries**, thereby causing heart disease.

If a piece of the fatty build up breaks away it can cause a blood clot to form. This **blocks the artery** as the heart is **deprived** of blood, causing a **heart attack**.

Dietary prevention
- reduce or replace saturated fat with polyunsaturated fats, e.g. margarine instead of butter
- have a diet high in ACE vitamins and unrefined carbohydrates

Lifestyle prevention
- be more physically active, this will reduce stress and expend more calories
- reduce/stop smoking
- reduce alcohol intake

Quick Test

1. Identify one dietary cause and one lifestyle cause of obesity and heart disease.
2. Explain how heart disease effects health.
3. How can obesity be prevented through diet?
4. John is a forty-year-old overweight man whose father recently died of a heart attack. Look at John's typical daily lunch: bottle of fizzy juice with a steak sandwich (steak fried in butter, cheddar cheese, mayonnaise, salt, all on a white baguette). **Identify** and **explain** any three dietary changes he could make to reduce his risk of heart disease.

Dietary diseases: high blood pressure, diabetes and dental caries

High blood pressure

Diet-related causes
- diet high in salt/sodium
- being overweight

Lifestyle-related causes
- stress
- high alcohol intake
- insufficient exercise

Other causes
- hereditary factors
- gender: men are more likely to suffer from HBP than women.
- increasing age

Effect on health

High blood pressure is usually caused by **narrowed/damaged arteries**. The heart has to work **extra hard to pump blood around the body**. This can increase the risk of a **stroke** or a **heart attack**.

It is often called the 'silent killer' as the majority of people suffer no symptoms at all.

Dietary prevention
- reduce intake of salt

Lifestyle prevention
- be more physically active; this will reduce stress and expend more calories
- reduce alcohol intake

Diabetes (Type 2)

Diet-related causes
- being overweight

Lifestyle-related causes
- stress
- insufficient exercise

Other causes
- ethnic origin

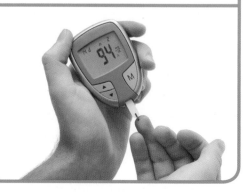

Effect on health

Insulin produced in the pancreas is used to regulate blood glucose levels. With Type 2 diabetes the insulin produced is no longer effective, and this prevents the body being able to regulate blood glucose after eating food. Type 2 diabetes affects millions of people world-wide.

Symptoms

- feeling unwell
- passing more urine
- feeling tired
- thirst

Dietary prevention

- eat a balanced diet

Lifestyle prevention

- be more physically active: exercise increases the body's ability to regulate blood glucose levels

> **TOP TIP**
>
> Remember, this is not a definitive list of diseases. You might also want to look into the effects of **cancer and constipation.**

Dental caries (tooth decay)

Diet-related causes

- diet high in sugars
- diet low in calcium, phosphorous and vitamin D

Lifestyle-related causes

- lack of knowledge about brushing teeth regularly

Effect on health

Sugar in foods feeds the bacteria in your mouth. Plaque is then formed, which causes tooth decay.

Dietary prevention

- choose raw vegetables, fruit and nuts as snacks
- reduce non-milk extrinsic (NME) sugar intake
- reduce amount of sugary drinks consumed

Lifestyle prevention

Good dental hygiene – ensure teeth are brushed twice a day with a fluoride toothpaste and visit a dentist regularly.

Quick Test

1. Identify one diet-related cause and one lifestyle-related cause of high blood pressure.
2. What are the main symptoms of diabetes?
3. Give a piece of advice to a parent on how to prevent their child getting tooth decay.
4. Explain how teeth can become decayed.

Dietary diseases: osteoporosis and anaemia

Osteoporosis

Diet-related causes
- diet low in calcium, phosphorus and Vitamin D
- diet high in NSP
- diet high in salt

Lifestyle-related causes
- lack of exercise
- smoking

Susceptible groups
- people with a low body weight
- the elderly

The word 'susceptible' means more likely to be influenced or harmed by a particular thing.

Effect on health
Each bone is made up of a thick outer shell and a strong inner mesh, which looks like honeycomb. Osteoporosis occurs when the inner mesh of the bone becomes thin and weak and as a consequence the bones become brittle and break easily.

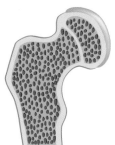
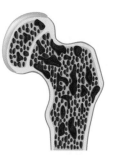

Healthy bone

Bone of an osteoporosis sufferer

Symptoms
Usually goes unnoticed until a minor fall or awkward movement leads to a fracture

Dietary prevention
- have a diet high in calcium, phosphorous and vitamin D, e.g. eat more dairy foods
- reduce salt intake – too much salt can lead to calcium loss in the bones

Lifestyle prevention
- increase the amount of weight-bearing exercise
- get enough exposure to sunlight, as this contains vitamin D, which absorbs calcium in the body
- avoid smoking

TOP TIP

Bones are usually fully formed by the age of 25. After this, the calcium intake only helps maintain bone health. So it is vital that a calcium-friendly diet is followed through childhood and adolescence.

Anaemia

Diet-related causes
- snacking or grazing
- diet low in vitamin B12
- diet low in iron and vitamin C
- diet low in folic acid

Lifestyle-related causes
Susceptible groups:
- vegetarians/vegans
- menstruating girls
- pregnant women
- teenagers
- boys going through a growth spurt
- babies

Effect on health
Iron deficiency anaemia occurs when there is insufficient iron in the body. As a consequence there is not enough **haemoglobin** in the red blood cells. Therefore it is difficult for oxygen to be transported around the body.

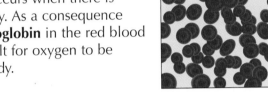

Normal red blood   Anaemic red blood
cell count   cell count

Symptoms
- pale skin
- tiredness
- breathlessness

Dietary prevention
- have a diet high in iron and vitamin C
- green leafy vegetables
- red meat
- citrus fruits

Lifestyle prevention
- increase the amount of weight-bearing exercise
- get enough exposure to sunlight, as this contains vitamin D, which absorbs calcium in the body
- avoid smoking

Quick Test

1. Which groups are most susceptible to osteoporosis?
2. How can osteoporosis be avoided?
3. Julie is a fifty-year-old vegetarian who has recently been feeling tired and breathless. Explain what dietary disease you think Julie might have. **Define** what this disease is.

Current dietary advice

Scottish dietary targets

Much of Scotland's poor health record can be attributed to its unhealthy eating habits. As a consequence, there are high levels of heart disease, cancer, hypertension, Type 2 diabetes and obesity in Scotland. The government has set out healthy eating guidelines to try and combat these diet-related diseases.

Eat more ...

Fruit and vegetables Intake to double to at least 400g per day. 	**Benefit to the body** • low in fat • contains the ACE vitamins **Dietary disease prevented** • weight gain/obesity • reduces risk of heart disease/some cancers **Meeting the target** • have a glass of orange juice with breakfast • have vegetable soup for lunch
Total complex carbohydrates Intake to increase by 25%. 	**Benefit to the body** • contains NSP • aids digestion/reduces constipation **Dietary disease prevented** • reduces risk of bowel disorders **Meeting the target** • have rice or pasta instead of chips • use wholemeal flour instead of white flour
Bread Intake to increase, mainly wholemeal, by 45%. 	**Benefit to the body** • contains NSP • aids digestion/reduces constipation **Dietary disease prevented** • reduces risk of bowel disorders **Meeting the target** • use wholemeal bread instead of white bread • use breadcrumbs to coat/bulk food items

 got it? ☐ ☐ ☑

Breakfast cereals
Intake to double to 34g per day.

Benefit to the body
- some are fortified with folic acid

Dietary disease prevented
- spina bifida in unborn babies

Meeting the target
- have a bowl of wholegrain cereal as a snack
- used crushed cereals as toppings for pies or desserts

Fish
Intake of oily fish to double to 88g per week.

Benefit to the body
- contains omega-3

Dietary disease prevented
- blood clots/heart disease

Meeting the target
- use fish instead of meat in a stir fry
- use oily fish as a topping on a pizza

Plus ...

Breastfeeding
Increase the number of mothers who breastfeed for at least the **first six weeks** of the baby's life.

Benefit to the body
- breast milk contains antibodies

Dietary disease prevented
- breast milk contains antibodies, which help fight infections and prevent allergies

TOP TIP

In the exam you could be asked to give practical examples of how you could meet one or more of the dietary targets. Make sure you know at least one practical example for each target.

Current dietary advice

Scottish dietary targets: eat less ...

Fat
Decrease intake of saturated fat to no more than 11% of food energy.

Benefit to the body
- lowers cholesterol

Dietary disease prevented
- reduces the risk of heart disease and cancer

Meeting the target
- swap animal fats for vegetable fats
- remove all visible fat off meat before cooking

Salt
Decrease intake to no more than 6g a day.

Benefit to the body
- lowers blood pressure

Dietary disease prevented
- reduces risk of hypertension and strokes

Meeting the target
- use herbs or spices to flavour food
- avoid processed foods

Sugar
Decrease intake of NME sugars in children by half to no more than 10% of energy.

Benefit to the body
- prevents the growth of plaque

Dietary disease prevented
- reduces risk of tooth decay

Meeting the target
- use dried fruit or honey to add sweetness to food items

TOP TIP
Always read food labels to identify whether the product helps meet the dietary targets.

got it? ☐ ☐ ☑

How food manufacturers are helping consumers to meet the dietary targets

Target	What are they doing to help consumers make informed choices?
Increase intake of fruit and vegetables	Manufacturers have a wider selection of fruit and vegetables. Many of these are already peeled and chopped to save the consumer time.
Increase intake of bread	Manufacturers have increased their selection of breads e.g. fresh bread baked on site, prepacked loaves and foreign breads like naan or focaccia. This gives the consumer a wider choice.
Increase intake of breakfast cereals	Manufacturers have increased their range of breakfast products, e.g. cereal bars and single-serving cereals with milk that are available in the chilled section. This is more convenient for the consumer who needs to eat on the go.
Increase intake of total complex carbohydrate	Manufacturers are incorporating more fruit and vegetables and wholegrains into their products.
Increase intake of fish	Many supermarkets have fish counters. This allows the consumer to buy fresh fish and get advice from the in-store fishmonger.
Reduce intake of fat	Manufacturers have increased their range of low-fat or slimmers' foods. This allows consumers to make an informed choice.
Reduce intake of salt	Manufacturers are reducing salt, by using herbs and spices to retain flavour.
Reduce intake of sugar	Manufacturers are using artificial sweeteners or sugar substitutes. This allows consumers to make an informed choice.

Quick Test

Look at the Scottish menu below.

> **Starter**
> Smoked salmon terrine with white crusty bread
>
> **Main course**
> Highland haggis, neeps and tatties
>
> **Dessert**
> Whisky and raspberry cranachan with homemade shortbread

1. Identify two changes that could be made to the menu to make them meet the dietary targets.
2. Explain what target is met by each change.
3. Explain one way that manufacturers are helping consumers increase their consumption of fruit and vegetables.

Ingredients and cooking methods

Retaining nutrients

To help you achieve current dietary advice it is equally important to choose the correct cooking method as the correct foods to eat. Some ways of cooking will result in a loss of vitamins from the food. In particular, the water-soluble vitamins are lost easily.

Effects of cooking on vitamins

TOP TIP

Use the water you have boiled vegetables in to make soup or sauces.

Heat
Vitamins B and C are both lost when heated.
Vitamin B is lost at temperatures **over boiling point**.
Vitamin C is lost at temperatures **lower than boiling point**.

Alkalinity
Vitamin B is reduced if baking powder is added.
Vitamin C is lost if bicarbonate of soda is added to the water when cooking.

Solubility
Vitamins B and C are both **lost in water** as they are water soluble. They **leach out** into the water or are lost if cooked for too long.

Cooking methods

Method	Analyse the cooking method and identify suitable foods	Evaluate if the cooking method contributes to a healthy diet
Grilling 	• quick method of cooking, which helps to retain the nutrients in the food • uses intense heat, which is radiated over food • meat, fish, vegetables	✓ little or no fat is added ✓ fat in the food melts and drips out ✓ target linked to = reduced intake of fat

Steaming 	• food is cooked in steam from boiling water • vegetables, fish, eggs, sweet or savoury puddings	✓ little or no fat is added ✓ fewer nutrients are lost as the food does not come in contact with water (e.g. the water-soluble nutrients are not leached) ✓ target linked to = reduced intake of fat
Stir-frying 	• quick cooking method, which cooks food in a small amount of oil at a high temperature • fish, meat, vegetables	✓ very little oil is used ✓ fewer nutrients are lost as the food is cooked ✓ target linked to = reduced intake of fat
Deep-fat frying 	• involves fully immersing food in hot oil • meat, vegetables, fruit, eggs, batters, doughs	✗ food is submerged and cooked in fat ✗ destroys some nutrients and essential fatty acids

Quick Test

1. List which vitamins are most easily lost through some cookery methods.
2. Choose two cookery methods and explain how they contribute to a healthy diet.
3. What method should be used to cook potatoes if you want to keep as many vitamins as possible?
4. Explain why deep fat frying does not contribute to a healthy diet.

Individual dietary needs: babies, toddlers and children

Understanding nutrition can be complicated because there are so many components and because **each person** has their own **individual needs**. Women's needs differ from those of men, and older women's needs differ from those of young girls. **As we age our needs constantly change** and therefore it is vital that you understand the different dietary groups and what their nutritional needs are.

Babies

Key information

A newborn or recently born infant. They grow rapidly during the first few weeks of life.

Their diet consists of mainly milk for at least the first six months of life.

Dietary/health needs

Breastfeeding (lactation):

Provides all the necessary nutrients in the correct proportions at the correct temperature. Also, the Scottish Dietary Target recommends that babies should be breastfed for at least the first six weeks of life. But why?

✓ helps create a bond between mother and baby

✓ contains nutrients (protein, fats, calcium) and antibodies that help to fight infections and prevent allergies and asthma

✓ free and convenient

✓ can help mother lose excess baby weight

✓ milk can be expressed so father/family can help

✗ can be difficult if the mother is intending to return to work quickly

✗ there is often a stigma attached to breastfeeding in public

✗ the father may feel left out

Bottle-feeding

✓ parents can share responsibility

✓ mother can return to work quickly

✗ cost of equipment/milk

✗ Preparation time

Other possible health issues

Babies can be **prone to infections** because they have weaker immune systems, so it is essential that all feeding products are **sterilised before use**.

TOP TIP

No salt or sugar should be added to weaning foods.

Between birth and four months babies cannot eat solid foods as they do not have the mouth and tongue movements necessary for swallowing. After this point a baby can be **weaned** on to solid foods.

The word 'weaned' means to introduce solid foods gradually into a baby's diet.

Toddlers and children

Children often mirror the eating patterns and behaviour of their parents/carers. It is vital that good eating habits are formed at an early age. A healthy balanced diet should be encouraged.

Key information
A child is a young human being below the age of puberty.

Dietary/health needs
During this period of rapid growth it is vital that children get protein to ensure their body tissues grow and repair properly. Calcium, phosphorous and vitamin D are needed for their bone and teeth development.

As children are usually very active, carbohydrate is needed to give them energy. They also need iron and vitamin C to create red blood cells so that oxygen is transported around the body, thereby preventing tiredness.

Other possible health issues
Constipation can be an issue due to the lack of fibre and fruit and vegetables in some children's diets.

Tips for creating good eating habits
- ✓ keep food colourful and attractive
- ✓ keep portions small and easy to swallow
- ✓ include a variety of flavours and textures
- ✓ encourage that meals are eaten at a dinner table, to enhance social skills

Quick Test

1. Give another name for lactation.
2. How long does the Scottish Dietary Target recommend that mothers breastfeed for?
3. Give one advantage and one disadvantage of breastfeeding and bottle-feeding.
4. Name the gradual introduction of solid food to a baby's diet.
5. Identify and explain three nutrients that are important in the diet of a child.

Individual dietary needs: teenagers and adults

Teenagers

A teenager's diet often reflects that of his or her family; however, it is also influenced by peer pressure and the media. Teenage girls often face the problem of developing unhealthy eating habits associated with dieting and slimming.

Key information

A teenager is a person between the ages of thirteen and nineteen; an adolescent.

Dietary/health needs

Growth spurts often occur during adolescence, so protein is required to ensure that teenagers' body tissues grow, are maintained and repair properly. Furthermore, calcium, phosphorous and vitamin D are needed for bone and teeth development.

There is an increased demand for energy, as teenage body frames change and grow, therefore adequate carbohydrates and vitamin B are required.

Similarly blood volume increases as we grow, so iron and vitamin C are required to ensure healthy blood. Teenage girls need to increase intake of these, especially when their periods start (menstruation).

As teenagers become more independent, they make more of their own food choices; therefore food education is important. Nutrition, cooking methods, preparation time, disadvantages of convenience foods, cost, eating patterns/cravings and physical activity are all topics that teenagers should be aware of. This will help them make **informed choices** when it comes to eating.

Other possible health issues

Teenagers can be prone to a number of deficiencies if they do not follow a healthy balanced diet:

- iron deficiency (anaemia)
- calcium deficiency.

TOP TIP

The World Health Organization (WHO) predicts that the next new epidemic in children and young adults will be Type 2 diabetes. This is as a direct result of inactivity and poor eating habits. Take responsibility for your health and stop this from happening.

Adults

During adulthood, people tend to be less active and, because body growth has stopped, energy needs decrease. Remember, to prevent weight gain, energy must balance.

Key information

An adult is a fully developed and mature grown-up.

Dietary/health needs

Adulthood should be a time for health maintenance, so it is important that adults get the appropriate amount of the following nutrients:

- Protein to ensure their body tissues are maintained and are repaired properly.
- Calcium, phosphorous and vitamin D are needed to maintain healthy bones and prevent osteoporosis.
- Carbohydrate intake should be balanced with an individual's energy expenditure.

Generally speaking, adults should eat little and often as this stabilises their blood sugar levels and keeps their metabolic rate consistent.

Other possible health issues

Adults should limit their intake of saturated fats as this will help to prevent the risk of **obesity** and **heart disease**.

Furthermore, they should reduce their intake of salt to prevent **high blood pressure**.

> ## TOP TIP
>
> When answering a question about individuals, remember the Scottish dietary targets and the eatwell plate give healthy eating recommendations to everyone over preschool age.

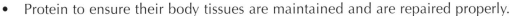

Quick Test

1. List the nutrients that are important for a menstruating teenage girl.
2. Identify and explain two nutrients that should be limited in the diet of an adult.
3. Identify a dietary disease that teenagers are prone to.
4. Explain why teenagers often make poor food choices.

Individual dietary needs: elderly people and pregnant women

Elderly people

The nutritional needs of the elderly are difficult to categorise neatly. Dietary needs depend on current health and, while many older people are fit and active, some others may be less active, frail and require additional care.

Key information

In most countries in the developed world 'elderly' means sixty-five-plus years of age.

Other factors that influence the food choices of elderly people are:

- limited budget
- lack of motivation
- loneliness
- immobility.

Dietary/health needs

As people age they tend to become less active. This means they expend less energy, therefore carbohydrate intake should be balanced with an individual's energy expenditure.

Other key nutrients include protein, which is required to ensure that body tissues are maintained and are repaired properly, especially in people who are convalescing (recovering from an illness).

Calcium, phosphorous and vitamin D are needed to maintain healthy bones and prevent osteoporosis and osteomalacia (soft bones).

Furthermore, the body's digestive system slows down with age, so NSP is required to help prevent bowel disorders.

Some elderly people have difficulty chewing, food should be of a softer texture, for example mashed potatoes instead of boiled. Food also should be quick and easy to prepare and be served in small manageable portions.

Other possible health issues

The elderly should limit their intake of saturated fats as this will help lower levels of cholesterol in the blood, helping to prevent heart disease.

They should reduce their intake of salt to prevent high blood pressure and the risk of a stroke.

Other common diseases:

- anaemia
- osteomalacia
- osteoporosis
- constipation.

TOP TIP

Many elderly people have long-term, or chronic, disorders, such as high blood pressure and arthritis, and need to take daily medications to control their symptoms. Some of these medications can block the absorption of the essential nutrients.

Pregnant women

A healthy diet can help women conceive, and when they become pregnant it helps support the development, wellbeing and future health of the baby. With a few exceptions, pregnant women can continue to eat normally before and during pregnancy.

Key information
Pregnancy is the period from conception to birth, which normally lasts approximately forty weeks.

Dietary/health needs
All nutrients are important during pregnancy, particularly **protein** as it helps to develop the body cells of the foetus. **Carbohydrate** is needed, especially in the last three months of pregnancy, which is a rapid growth period for the baby. **NSP** and water are important in the diet as constipation can be an issue for pregnant women.

A good supply of **iron** and **vitamin C** is essential as the baby stores the iron during pregnancy to be used during the first four months of life.

Folic acid intake is advised before becoming pregnant and for the first three months. This helps to reduce the risk of the baby being born with spina bifida.

Other possible health issues

Mother

- constipation
- infections (caused by a lowered immune system)
- obesity

Developing foetus

- spina bifida
- overweight

Pregnant women should avoid the following as they can harm the developing foetus:

✗ alcohol – it leads to poor nutrient absorption

✗ smoking – it can lead to a low birth weight

✗ raw eggs – they could contain salmonella

✗ liver – it contains high levels of vitamin A

✗ soft ripened cheeses – they could contain listeria

Obesity can cause problems both with becoming pregnant and during pregnancy. Overweight women may have difficulty conceiving and they are at a higher risk of having a premature birth. Babies born of obese mothers are more prone to health problems later in life, including obesity and diabetes.

Quick Test

1. Name two diseases that the elderly may be prone to. What nutrients can help to prevent these?

2. Match the following statements.

Spina bifida can be caused by …	… vitamin A, which is harmful to the developing foetus.
A unborn born baby stores …	… lack of folic acid in the diet.
Liver contains high levels of …	… its mother's iron and uses it in the first four months of life.

Dietary reference values (DRVs)

Why are they needed?

DRVs are important for ensuring that an adequate intake of energy and nutrients occurs throughout our lives. Many health concerns and illnesses are linked to malnutrition. The DRVs assist in preventing malnutrition.

> Malnutrition is a serious condition that occurs when a person's diet does not contain enough nutrients to meet the demands of their body. Malnutrition can also be caused by eating too much of a nutrient.

DRV categories

These values are used in assessing the diets of groups of people. There are four categories of dietary reference value.

- **Estimated average requirement (EAR)** – The estimated average requirement for food energy or a nutrient. Many people will need more than this value, and many will need less.
- **Reference nutrient intake (RNI)** – The amount of a nutrient that is enough for almost every individual, even someone with high needs for that nutrient.
- **Lower reference nutrient intake (LRNI)** – The amount of a nutrient that is enough for only a small number of people with low needs. People regularly eating less than the LRNI are likely to be deficient.
- **Safe intake** – The amount of a nutrient that is judged adequate for almost everyone's needs, but is small enough not to cause undesirable effects. It is used where there is not enough information to estimate the requirements for that nutrient.

DRVs for different individuals

Each of the groups from pages 34 to 39 – babies, toddlers, children, adults, pregnant women and the elderly – has its own DRVs for each nutrient. These are the DRVs for teenage girls aged 15–18.

Dietary reference values for teenage girls aged 15–18					
Estimated average requirements	Reference nutrient intake				
Energy (MJ)	Protein (g)	Fibre (g)	Vitamin B1 (mg)	Vitamin C (mg)	Iron (g)
8·83	55·25	18	0·8	40	14·8

TOP TIP

For each individual group, ensure you know what specific needs they may have for each nutrient to help you answer questions about DRVs.

TOP TIP

There will always be a question about DRVs in the exam. See pages 103–104 for guidance on how to answer this type of question.

Quick Test

1. Match the first two columns and then write a definition of each DRV category.

Abbreviation	Name	Definition
RNI	Lower reference nutrient intake	
EAR	Reference nutrient intake	
LRNI	Estimated average requirement	

2. What category is missing from the table?

3. What condition do the DRVs help to prevent?

Food allergies vs food intolerances

How to tell the difference

A genuine food allergy occurs only rarely, with about 2% of the population affected. Food intolerance is more common. Allergy UK estimates that up to 45% of people in the UK suffer from food intolerance symptoms, including migraines, skin rashes and digestive problems.

Food allergy
- Symptoms come on within seconds or minutes of eating the food.
- In extreme cases the reaction can be life-threatening.
- Even a tiny trace of the food can cause a reaction.
- Food allergy is easily diagnosed with tests.

Food intolerance
- Symptoms come on more slowly and are long-lasting. They mainly involve the digestive system.
- It is never life-threatening.
- A reasonable portion of food is usually needed to cause a reaction, although some people can be sensitive to small amounts.
- You may crave the problem food.
- Food intolerance is difficult to diagnose as there are only a few reliable tests.

Food allergies

A food allergy is when the body's immune system reacts abnormally to specific foods. Allergic reactions are often mild, but they can sometimes be very serious. Common allergenic foods include nuts, shellfish, eggs and milk.

There is no treatment to cure a food allergy. The best way of preventing an allergic reaction is to identify the type of food that causes the allergy and then avoid it. People with a food allergy often carry an epi-pen, which contains dosages of adrenaline that can be used in case of an anaphylactic shock (a sudden, severe **allergic** reaction).

Labelling
People with food allergies have to be extremely careful about what they eat. Current food labelling rules set out that the inclusion of the following fourteen food allergens must be stated on the label: cereals containing gluten, crustaceans, molluscs, eggs, fish, peanuts, nuts, soybeans, milk, celery, mustard, sesame, lupin and sulphur dioxide.

Food intolerance

This occurs when the body is unable to deal with a certain type of foodstuff. This is usually because the body does not produce enough of the chemical or enzyme that is needed for digestion of that food.

What	Why	How
Lactose 	Lactose intolerance is a common digestive problem where the body is unable to digest lactose, a type of sugar mainly found in milk and dairy products. Symptoms include: • bloated stomach • flatulence (passing wind) • diarrhoea.	Lactose substitutes are available: • rice milk • soya milk. Drops are available that can be added to food or drink to improve digestion of lactose.
Gluten	Gluten sensitivity ranges from a mild intolerance to coeliac disease. Gluten is a protein found in the cereals wheat, rye and barley. In coeliac disease the immune system mistakes substances found inside gluten as a threat to the body and attacks them. This damages the surface of the small bowel (intestines), disrupting the body's ability to absorb nutrients from food. Eating foods containing gluten can trigger a range of symptoms, such as: • diarrhoea – which may be particularly unpleasant smelling • bloating and flatulence (passing wind) • abdominal pain • weight loss or weight gain.	There is no cure for coeliac disease. The only effective treatment for this disorder is a gluten-free diet. Anyone diagnosed with coeliac disease can receive foods such as bread, pasta, and flour mixes on prescription from their doctor. There are a wide variety of alternative gluten-free products now available from a variety of different manufacturers. Foods available vary but can include specially manufactured breads, pasta, flour and bread mixes, pizza bases, crackers and oats.

Quick Test

1. List two facts about food allergies.
2. List two facts about food intolerances.
3. State two common food intolerances.
4. What type of diet helps to treat coeliac disease?

New food products

The average household spends around **£5000** a year on food products. In supermarkets consumers have around **50 000 food products** to choose from. Food manufacturers are constantly developing new food products to ensure they get their share of the money you are spending on food.

From farm to supermarket

Where do the products on our supermarket shelves come from? The table below shows some examples of the journey our food makes from the farm to supermarket shelves.

Farming in the UK and other countries		Primary food processing Raw foods are made into foods that can be eaten by consumers		Secondary food processing Food manufacturers convert raw ingredients from primary processing into food products, often adding other ingredients
Fruit and vegetables	→	Cleaning of fruit and vegetables	→	Juicing apples to make apple juice
Crops (wheat, oats, etc.)	→	Milling wheat into flour	→	Making bread from flour
Dairy	→	Pasteurising milk	→	Turning milk into cheese
Meat (beef, pork, chicken, lamb, etc.)	→	Jointing a meat carcass	→	Using raw beef to make individual lasagna meals
Fish	→	Gutting a fish	→	Making mackerel into pâté

At the **secondary food processing** stage food manufacturers will try and make their product original, to stand out from the others on the supermarket shelves. Food manufacturers will also consider the **functional properties** of individual ingredients to make the best product (see pages 54–59).

TOP TIP

When food products are mentioned in the exam, think about what ingredients have been combined to make them – this will help you think about the nutrients that are in the product and why it has been developed.

Why are there so many new food products?

New food products give consumers increased choice when they are shopping, but remember food manufacturers want to make money from you. Below are some of the reasons why new food products have been developed.

Food for health (see pages 8–41)	Contemporary food issues (see pages 62–99)
To meet specific needs: coeliac disease, allergies, diabetes	Snacking
Dietary goals: less fat, salt, sugar; more fruit and vegetables, fish, total complex carbohydrates, bread, breakfast cereals	Vegetarian diets
	Technological developments
	Children's food ranges
Added nutrients: omega-3	Single portions
To prevent dietary diseases: constipation, CHD	Fairtrade ingredients
	Organic foods
For specific groups: babies, children, vegetarians	Price consumers willing to pay
	Foreign travel
	Consumers' practical skills
	Working patterns
	Less use of factory farming
	Sustainability
	Less packaging
	Use of functional foods

Quick Test

1. A new salmon-and-chive sandwich has been developed by a food manufacturer. List the main ingredients that would have been used and then identify where they would have come from.

2. List four new food products you have recently seen advertised or in a supermarket.

3. For the new products in question 2 identify a reason why each might have been developed by the food manufacturer.

Stages of food product development

Stage	Explanation	Example: a food manufacturer developing a new sandwich
1. Concept generation	The 'thinking stage' – where all ideas are considered for the new food product. Ideas may be developed from market research, identifying a gap in the market.	• survey of existing sandwiches the company produces and competitors' sandwiches • look at ingredients, cost, portion size, shelf-life • types of bread: wholemeal, white, wrap, pitta, baguette, roll • types of fillings: protein (duck, egg, cheese, chicken, etc.) • themes – healthy, international, etc. • survey consumers to find out what they like/dislike in a sandwich • disassemble competitors' sandwiches to discover quantities of ingredients
2. Concept screening	During this stage all the ideas from concept generation are looked over, some are kept and others are discarded. This information is then used to produce a specification that will allow the new food product to be developed.	Some specification points for the new sandwich: • will be made using a wrap: a questionnaire showed this is what consumers wanted and there are less filled wraps than other sandwiches currently on the market • will be sold for no more than £2.50: consumer survey stated this was acceptable maximum price • will contain no less than 50g of duck filling: in the disassembly all proteins were over 50g, duck was the least used meat and is popular with consumers.
3. Prototype production	A sample (prototype) of the new food product is developed.	The recipe is adapted: less duck is used as it is too expensive, additional spring onions are added instead.
	This prototype is tested and can be modified/adapted.	The new duck wrap is made in the test kitchen.

4. Product testing	Sensory testing is carried out to get consumers' opinions.	Consumers carry out a rating test of the duck wrap.
	Changes can still be made to the new food product.	Consumers felt the wrap was too dry so 10ml of additional hoisin sauce was added (the final product was then retested and found to be acceptable).
5. First production run	The new food product is trialled in the factory for the first time to check it can be manufactured in bulk.	The duck wrap is produced in bulk in the sandwich factory. Some filling fell out so the folding of the wrap was amended.
6. Marketing plan	The marketing team will plan how to ensure the new food product sells as well as possible – they will consider the 4Ps: • product: how will the new product be packaged? • place: where will the new food product be sold? • price: what will the cost be? • promotion: will there be any offers to attract consumers?	The duck wrap will be: • packaged in a tube to keep the wrap together while eating • sold in small city supermarkets as they sell more sandwiches than larger stores • sold for £2.50; this is a high price indicating a high-quality product • launched on social networking site, advertising free tasting sessions in stores.
7. Product launch	Consumers can now buy the new food product; sales of the new food product will be closely monitored.	The duck wrap is now on sale in only small city supermarkets in Glasgow and Edinburgh. If sales are good it will be rolled out across the UK.

> **TOP TIP**
>
> Write out the seven stages of product development on separate cards, shuffle them and see if you can put them in the correct order. Make sure you can explain at least one point at each stage.

Quick Test

1. Think of a different food and come up with some ideas of how you would develop that new food product.

2. Name the stage when each of the following activities would take place during the food product development: (a) sensory testing a new range of square pizzas; (b) the decision to sell a new mango, raspberry and orange smoothie in local shops; (c) investigating a range of soups currently on sale in supermarkets; (d) trialling a new chicken lasagna in bulk.

3. Give examples of what you would have in your marketing plan if promoting one of the new products in question 2.

Sensory evaluation

What is sensory evaluation?

Sensory evaluation measures a taster's opinion of the appearance, aroma, taste, texture and overall acceptability of food and drinks. Food manufacturers regularly use sensory evaluation throughout the product development process to find out consumers' opinions of new products.

Examples of sensory tests

1. Ranking test
Tasters are asked to rank foods in order of preference or in order of a characteristic (see sensory words).
This can be used by food manufacturers to:
- find out acceptability of new products to tasters
- find out why one food product is more popular than another.

2. Rating test
Tasters are given a scale and asked to rate the product for a characteristic (see sensory words) or preference.
This can be used by food manufacturers to:
- collect information about specific characteristics
- discover if a new food product has met the specification.

3. Paired comparison test
Tasters are asked to compare two samples for preference or a characteristic (see sensory words).
This can be used by food manufacturers to:
- find out which prototype tasters prefer
- find out if tasters notice changes made to a food product/recipe, e.g. reduced fat/salt.

4. Profiling test
Tasters rate a number of characteristics (see sensory words) of a food product.
This can be used by food manufacturers to:
- compare similar products to find out about competitors' products
- assess overall acceptability.

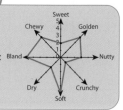

Here are some examples of **sensory words** that could be used in a sensory test or by tasters – some words can go in more than one category.

Appearance	Aroma	Taste	Texture	Overall acceptability
Golden	Spicy	Sweet	Short	Attractive
Pale	Sweet	Salty	Smooth	Colourful
Smooth	Yeasty	Spicy	Crisp	Shelf life

Checklist for carrying out sensory evaluation

Task	✓	Reason
Has excellent hygiene been used when setting up the sensory test?		To ensure that all samples have not been contaminated with bacteria.
Are there enough clean spoons and bowls/plates for each tester?		To prevent bacteria being transferred from taster to taster.
Have all samples been served identically (same size and temperature, etc.).		To allow tasters to compare each food fairly.
Have all samples been labelled with random letters/numbers?		To ensure tasters cannot identify each sample.
Is there a separate area/booth for each taster?		To ensure tasters are not influenced by each other.
Are there tasting charts at each area/booth?		To complete immediately so the taster does not forget what they thought.
Is there water/dry biscuits in each booth for tasters to use between tastings?		To remove any taste of a previous sample before tasting the next, giving more accurate results.
Do any tasters have any dietary needs or allergies?		To ensure that tasters with a food allergy or dietary need do not consume foods they shouldn't.
Check that all tasters are well and free from illness.		To avoid spread of infection between tasters and ensure accurate tasting results as illness can affect senses.
Is there a maximum of six samples per taster?		Taste buds will be less efficient if more samples are tasted.

TOP TIP

Whenever you eat a food product think what words you would use to describe it in a sensory test.

Quick Test

1. What would a food manufacturer be looking to find out if they carry out a profiling test of their existing tomato soup and similar products from their competitors?

2. Give two reasons a food manufacturer would carry out sensory testing.

3. When developing a new cake a food manufacturer develops two prototypes. What sensory test could they use to find out which prototype was the sweetest?

4. Name sensory words that could be used in a sensory test for the following foods:
   (a) apples; (b) salt and vinegar crisps; (c) custard; (d) ice cream; (e) fruit smoothie.

5. Why should tasters who are ill not be used to carry out a sensory test?

Hygienic practices

Bacteria

Bacteria are found everywhere and are so small that they cannot be seen on food. There are two types of bacteria found on food: spoilage and pathogenic.

Spoilage bacteria These cause food to go off.	**Pathogenic bacteria** These cause food poisoning.

Occurs when fruit and vegetables start to decay, meat goes slimy, etc.	An unpleasant illness caused by contaminated food that is eaten. Symptoms are diarrhoea, vomiting and abdominal pain.

In the majority of cases raw foods that come from animals contain bacteria, for example in the UK, chickens and eggs may contain the **pathogenic** bacteria *Salmonella*.

Food manufacturers want to prevent food spoilage to save waste and money.

When any food manufacturer develops food products, they must ensure that they are aware of when pathogenic bacteria may **contaminate** food and put steps in place to minimise the risk of consumers getting food poisoning.

Cross-contamination

Cross-contamination occurs when pathogenic bacteria transfer from one food to other foods by:

- **direct contact** – bacteria can be transferred from raw meat and fish if it touches food during storage
- **dripping** – bacteria can drip from raw meats and fish onto foods, which may not be cooked, if stored above other foods in a fridge
- **food workers** – food workers have bacteria in their hair, nose and hands, which can be transferred when they touch food. Food workers may touch raw meat, which has bacteria, and then touch other food/equipment without washing their hands
- **equipment and work surfaces** – bacteria can be transferred if raw food is prepared on a work surface/chopping board and the same area is then used to prepare food that is not going to be cooked.

Cross-contamination can be prevented by following rules in all areas of food production to ensure that anyone working in the food industry has high standards of **personal hygiene** and **kitchen hygiene**.

Personal hygiene	Reason
Hair must be tied back and covered.	Prevents bacteria on the hair falling into food.
A clean apron or overall must always be worn.	Prevents bacteria from clothes transferring to food.
All jewellery must be removed.	Prevents bacteria found in jewellery transferring to food.
All cuts must be covered with a blue waterproof plaster.	Prevents bacteria found in a cut transferring to food. A blue plaster can be clearly seen if it falls off while preparing food.
Anyone who is ill should not handle food.	Prevents bacteria from coughing or the illness transferring to food and other workers.
Hands must be washed before preparing food and regularly throughout production, especially after touching nose, hair or going to the toilet.	Prevents bacteria being on the hands and transferred to food that the worker touches. There should be no nail varnish worn as bacteria will settle in any chips and transfer to food.

Kitchen hygiene	Reason
Keep separate fridges for raw and cooked foods (if there is only one fridge the bottom shelf should be used for raw foods only).	Prevents bacteria transferring to cooked foods by direct contact or dripping.
All work surfaces are cleaned before preparing food and regularly throughout production with hot water and detergent.	Prevents bacteria transferring from the work surface to any food being prepared.
All food preparation equipment should be clean before use.	Prevents bacteria being transferred to fresh food.
Separate chopping boards/utensils for raw and cooked foods.	Prevents bacteria transferring to foods via the equipment.
All waste should be disposed off in covered buckets.	Prevents any pests or animals coming into the kitchen and spreading bacteria.
Ensure all fruit and vegetables are washed prior to use.	Prevents any bacteria from the soil/farming to contaminate the food. being produced.
Kitchen cloths should be changed regularly.	Prevents bacteria multiplying in a moist environment and transferring to food.

Quick Test

1. Explain the difference between spoilage and pathogenic bacteria.
2. List two symptoms of food poisoning.
3. Define the term cross-contamination.
4. Explain why regular hand washing is one of the most important personal hygiene rules.

Conditions for bacterial growth

Food manufacturers must take into account the **conditions for bacterial growth** to ensure that ingredients and food products have as long a shelf life as possible and to prevent outbreaks of food poisoning.

To prevent food poisoning and food spoilage bacteria multiplying, one of the conditions of bacterial growth must be removed.

What food manufacturers could do to prevent bacteria multiplying

Chilling, **freezing** or **cooking** food will prevent food spoiling, and killing bacteria when cooking will prevent food poisoning.

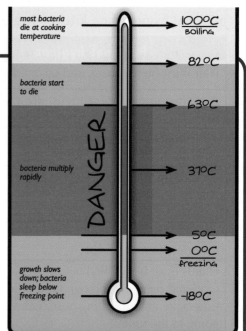

most bacteria die at cooking temperature	100°C BOILING
	82°C
bacteria start to die	63°C
bacteria multiply rapidly	37°C
	5°C
	0°C freezing
growth slows down; bacteria sleep below freezing point	−18°C

DANGER

Storage	Cooking
• All chilled foods should be stored at 1–4°C as soon as possible after purchase/delivery. • All frozen foods should be stored at −18°C as soon as possible after purchase/delivery. • When chilled/frozen ingredients are delivered, temperature checks should be carried out. • Temperature checks should be carried out when chilled frozen foods are delivered and regularly thereafter to ensure that fridges and freezers are operating at the correct temperature.	• All food must be thoroughly cooked to 75°C for at least 2 minutes – a temperature probe should be used. • All foods being reheated must be cooked to 82°C – a temperature probe should be used. 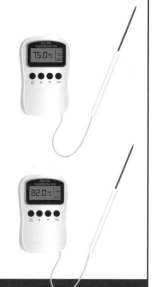
Other storage facts	**Other cooking facts**
• Raw and cooked foods should be stored in separate fridges. • All foods not stored in a fridge/freezer should be stored in a cool, dry place.	• If food is not being eaten straightaway after cooking it should be cooled quickly before being stored at 0–4°C.

TOP TIP

Know your temperatures: danger zone **5–63°C**; food must be cooked to **75°C**; food must be reheated to **82°C**; fridges should be at **1–4°C**, freezers should be **−18°C**.

What food manufacturers can do to prevent bacteria multiplying	
Time	• As bacteria will divide in two every twenty minutes, all food should be used as **quickly** as possible and definitely within the use-by date. • Food should not be left in the **danger zone** for long periods of time.
Oxygen	• **Aerobic** bacteria need oxygen to grow while anaerobic bacteria can multiply without oxygen. • When foods have been **sealed**, for example in a tin, they should be treated as fresh food once opened, as oxygen will now be present. • Where possible, all foods should be **covered**.
Moisture	• Most foods contain water so bacteria will multiply. • **Drying** foods removes moisture, extending the shelf life of foods such as pasta and raisins. • All foods should be stored in dry conditions to prevent bacteria multiplying in foods such as flour and rice.
Neutral pH	• Adding an **acid** such as vinegar to certain ingredients can preserve them and make them last longer. This is because the neutral pH has been removed, e.g. pickled onions, pickled eggs.
Food	• Bacteria will multiply best on meat and dairy products, as they have a high protein content, and fruits, which have high water contents. • High-risk foods – in particular meat and dairy products which will not be reheated – must be stored at the correct temperature.

TOP TIP

Bacterial growth can be slowed down or prevented if conditions are changed or removed.

Quick Test

1. What temperature is the danger zone?
2. Explain why it is dangerous to leave food in the danger zone.
3. Why should cooked foods not be put straight into the fridge?
4. Identify which condition for bacterial growth is removed in the following examples:
   (a) As soon as ham was used to make a sandwich it was returned to the fridge.
   (b) Bags of flour and rice are stored on a shelf in a dry cupboard.
   (c) A new chutney has been developed using tomatoes, onions and vinegar.
   (d) Frozen chicken that was delivered was stored immediately in the freezer.

Functional properties of eggs and sugar

Eggs are a versatile ingredient in food production as they have three distinct functions that can be used in a variety of ways.

Coagulation	Aeration	Emulsifying
When eggs are heated the protein **coagulates**, turning the liquid egg into a solid.	When eggs are whisked they trap **air**; this air will then expand when heated, causing baked goods to rise.	When egg yolk is added to oil and vinegar the lecithin found in the yolk allows the ingredients to **mix** without separating.

When eggs are heated the protein **coagulates**, turning the liquid egg into a solid.

Coagulation also allows the following properties:

- **Binding:** eggs can be added to **bind** ingredients together. When cooked the egg **coagulates**, keeping the ingredients together:
  - burgers, fish cakes, biscuits.

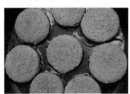

- **Glazing:** beaten egg can be brushed onto food products, which when heated will **coagulate**, colouring the food product:
  - scones, pastry.

Examples of coagulation:

- boiled, fried, poached, scrambled egg or omelette
- egg custard/quiche – the egg thickens/sets the mixture
- baked products, e.g. cakes, the egg gives structure

When eggs are whisked they trap **air**; this air will then expand when heated, causing baked goods to rise.

> **TOP TIP**
>
> Do not overcook eggs: boiled, poached and fried eggs will become rubbery.

Examples of aeration:

- meringues – egg whites whisked
- whisked sponge – egg and sugar whisked together

When egg yolk is added to oil and vinegar the lecithin found in the yolk allows the ingredients to **mix** without separating.

> **TOP TIP**
>
> Do not use eggs straight out of a fridge for baking. When they are at room temperature they will incorporate more air. If you forget to take them out of the fridge, put them in a bowl of warm water for ten minutes.

Examples of emulsifying:

- mayonnaise – is an emulsion of oil and vinegar

Sugar

Sugar's main use in food products is to add sweetness. However there are two other functional properties of sugar that can be used when manufacturing foods.

Crystallisation

When sugar and water are boiled the water is driven off, leaving a thick syrup. Crystals will form as the liquid cools → **crystallisation**.

- This process used in confectionary to make boiled sweets, fudge, tablet, etc.
- To prevent crystals forming when they are not wanted, the correct proportion of sugar needs to be used. For example, crystals in jam would result in a gritty texture.

Caramelisation

When sugar is heated to a high temperature it will turn brown and taste like toffee.

- Caramelisation is used in confectionery. When cakes are baked the sugar is heated and turns brown, colouring the crust.
- Sugar can be added to the tops of products then heated and caramelised, e.g. crème brûlé (right).

Changing the quantity of sugar in food products

Less sugar	More sugar
pale colour	dark colour
less flavour	sweeter product
cake will not rise as well	cakes will have a hard crust

TOP TIP

Do not overheat sugar as the caramel will become too dark and taste bitter.

Quick Test

1. State which functional property of eggs is used to make the following food products:
    (a) burgers
    (b) quiche
    (c) mayonnaise
    (d) meringues.
2. What will happen when beaten egg is brushed over the top of scones?
3. Give two food products that use crystallisation.
4. What will happen to the colour of a cake if the sugar content is reduced?

Functional properties of fats and flours

Fats

Fat is a very useful ingredient when cooking foods as it adds **flavour** to food products and helps to **increase shelf life**.

Shortening	Aeration	Glazing
When fat (butter or margarine) is rubbed into flour the fat coats the flour (waterproofing it), preventing the flour from absorbing water. This stops the dough becoming elastic and gives a **short** crumbly texture.	When fat (butter or margarine) is **creamed** or **rubbed in**, air can become trapped, causing foods to rise. **Creaming** When butter or margarine and castor sugar are creamed together with either an electric whisk or wooden spoon, the mixture will contain tiny bubbles of air. **Rubbing in** When fat is rubbed into flour and the hands are raised, air is trapped as the mixture falls back into the bowl.	When fat (butter or margarine) is added to cooked vegetables it will melt, giving a shiny glazed finish. When fat (butter or margarine) is added to sauces it will help make the sauce shine. Lack of fat will give sauces a dull finish.

TOP TIP

Be able to explain how the functional properties of each ingredient may affect different food products: for example, by putting too much flour in a sauce it will become very thick.

Examples of shortening:

- shortbread
- biscuits
- shortcrust pastry

Examples of aeration:

- creamed sponge cakes
- scones

Examples of glazing:

- peas, carrots potatoes, etc.
- sauces

TOP TIP

Go to this website and complete the interactive 'overview of the functional properties of food' in the 1–16 section. http://www.foodafactoflife.org.uk

Flour

Gelatinisation	Dextrinisation	Fermentation
Occurs when a liquid is **thickened** by heating it with a starch, e.g. wheat flour or cornflour. As the mixture is heated the starch molecules absorb the liquid and then swell to five times their size and burst, thickening the liquid.	Occurs when foods containing flour are cooked using dry heat (toaster, grill, oven). The starch in the flour will change to **dextrin**, causing the food to turn brown.	Occurs when yeast produces carbon dioxide and alcohol. Flour becomes the food that yeast requires in bread making. The natural sugars present in flour are **fermented** by the yeast when left in warmth, then carbon dioxide and alcohol are produced, raising the dough.
Examples of gelatinisation: • custard • white sauce • cheese sauce The thickness of the end product will depend on the amount of flour used. 	**Examples of dextrinisation:** • toast • baked goods – cakes, scones etc. 	**Examples of fermentation:** • bread making 

Quick Test

1. What functional properties do fats contribute to all foods?
2. Explain one way fat can contribute to air being added to foods.
3. Describe the different colours that bread can become when it is cooked under a grill.
4. Explain why biscuits have a crumbly texture.
5. When baking a cake explain a functional property of both fat and flour.

Functional properties of liquids

A variety of liquids can be **added** to food products. Liquids can also be used to **cook** foods as the heat is transferred through the liquid to the food being cooked. For example, boiling carrots in water, poaching fish in milk, boiling vegetables in stock for soup.

Any liquid used will increase the volume of a food product. However, if it is heated, the water in the liquid will start to evaporate. The volume will therefore decrease.

Liquid	How can these liquids be used in a recipe?
Water: has no flavour or nutritional value. The liquids below all contain water.	• to **bind** dry ingredients to make pastry, biscuits, hamburgers, etc. • to add **volume** to drinks, soups and sauces • to work with starch to **thicken** sauces (gelatinisation) • in baking to produce steam, helping cakes to **rise** • when making bread to give yeast the moisture to produce CO_2 gas in the dough

Milk: cow, goat, soya, etc.	• adds nutrients and **flavour** and can be used to:
	  – **glaze** baked goods, e.g. scones
	  – **caramelise** – milk contains natural sugars that when heated can change the colour of the food product
	  – **poach** foods, e.g. fish, and the milk can then be used to make a flavoursome sauce.
	• When heating milk it should always be stirred, otherwise a skin will form on top of the milk, which can spoil a product.

Stock: beef, fish vegetable, chicken, etc.	• Stock can be used to:
	  – add a concentrated **flavour** to products, e.g. beef stock in a bolognaise, vegetable stock in a soup
	  – add a **salty flavour** to foods.

Functional properties of ingredients in food products

TOP TIP

Remember, each ingredient may have more than one function in a recipe.

The examples below show how many functional properties of ingredients are used when manufacturing a product. Most ingredients have more than one function in the same recipe.

The functional properties of ingredients in a cake

Flour (50g)
- The protein in the flour will **coagulate**, giving the cake structure.

Eggs (50g)
- The protein in the egg will **coagulate**, giving the cake structure.
- The protein in the eggs will **trap air** when the cake mixture is whisked so help the cake **rise**.

Margarine (50g)
- The fat in the margarine will add **flavour** to the cake.
- The fat in the margarine will also help increase the **shelf-life** of the cake.
- When creamed together with sugar it will **trap air**, helping help the cake to **rise**.

Sugar (50g)
- Will add **sweetness** to the cake.
- When the cake is baked the sugar will **caramelise** giving a golden colour to the cake.
- When creamed together with margarine, the mixture will **trap air**. This will help the cake to **rise**.

The functional properties of ingredients in macaroni cheese

Flour (25g)
- The flour will absorb the milk and when heated the starch granules will burst, **thickening** the sauce **(gelatinisation)**.

Polyunsaturated margarine (25g)
- Add flavour to the sauce.
- Add **shine** to the sauce.

Low fat cheddar cheese (50g)
- Will **melt** when added to the hot sauce, causing the sauce to **thicken** further.
- Add **some flavour** to the sauce. As it is low in fat, it will have less flavour than full-fat cheese.

Semi-skimmed milk (250ml)
- Will be absorbed by the flour.
- Will provide **bulk** for the quantity of sauce required.

Quick Test

1. Identify three functional properties of milk.
2. What are the three functions of sugar when making a cake?
3. You have developed a new pasta sauce using margarine, flour, milk and cheese. The sauce is too thick. Which ingredients could you change the quantity of to make the sauce thinner?
4. Explain what would happen to the pasta sauce if chicken stock was used instead of milk.

Proportion of ingredients

Changing the proportion of ingredients will affect the finished product. This is an important factor to consider in food product development, especially if food manufacturers are trying to reduce fat and sugar for health reasons.

Ingredient	↑ Effect of an increase in a recipe	↓ Effect of a reduction in a recipe
Fat	• increases flavour • colour will be darker • cakes – will be softer and greasier • scones – will be more cake-like • pastry – greasy, more crumbly • sauces – will taste fatty	• less flavour • colour will be paler • baked goods will not last as long • scones – will be harder • pastry – will be harder • sauces – will not have shiny appearance
Sugar	• colour will be darker • increased sweetness • will need to cook foods for longer • scones – will look speckled • sauces – will be thin and runny • cakes – will have hard sugary crust • fruit will sink to the bottom • cake – will sink in the middle	• colour will be paler • lack of flavour • cakes – will not rise as much
Liquids	• top of the cake will crack • fruit will sink to the bottom of a cake • hard pastry • bread dough – too sticky • scone dough – will be too soft and scones will not keep their shape when cooked	• cakes – will be dry • scones – will not rise as well • pastry – will be crumbly and difficult to roll out • bread – will not rise as well and will be heavy

TOP TIP

In the exam you may be given examples of food products that have not worked out as expected, e.g. a scone which is hard. Use the information in this table to help you explain why that happened.

got it? ☐ ☐ ☑

Choosing ingredients

TOP TIP
The correct cooking time and method are as important as the ingredients used.

When developing a new recipe it is important to think about what texture, colour, smell, shape, flavour, etc. you want your end food product to be and to consider what ingredients might help you do this.

Fruit and vegetables come in a **variety of colours** so can be chosen to add colour to a dish.

Herbs and spices can be added to improve both the **flavour** and **smell** of foods.

Pastas are produced in a variety of **shapes**; some will hold sauces, e.g. twists (fusilli), while lasagna is good for layering.

Wholemeal flour will add a different **texture** and a nutty flavour compared to other flours.

Strong flour has more gluten, which forms the structure of baked goods and is better for bread.

When an egg white is whisked it will double in volume.

Beans and pulses come in a variety of colours and sizes.

Adding air – air can be added by hand or using electrical equipment such as a food processor or an electric whisk.

Ingredients

White, brown and demerara sugars will give different **colours** to the end-products.

Grilling foods will remove some of the fat, changing the texture of foods, e.g. bacon.

Baking foods can give a crisp texture.

Fresh ingredients are more expensive than frozen or canned ingredients.

The size and shape of vegetables can change how a food product will look.

Baking foods will change the colour from pale to darker the longer it is in the oven.

Vegetable preparation – vegetables can be prepared by hand using vegetable/cooks' knives or using food processors.

Quick Test

1. What change to ingredients could cause a cake to sink in the middle?

2. Match the following statements.

(i) Reducing sugar in a recipe.	A. Pastry will be crumbly and difficult to roll out.
(ii) Increasing fat in a recipe.	B. Cakes will not rise as much.
(iii) Too little liquid in a recipe.	C. Scones will be more cake-like.

3. Which method of cooking would ensure green beans kept their colour during cooking?

4. Look at the results for the sensory testing of a scone and suggest how a food manufacturer could amend the recipe to increase the flavour (flour, sugar, margarine, milk, raisins).

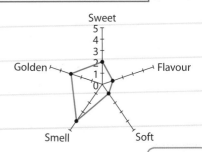

Factors affecting consumer food choice 1

There are many issues that affect the purchases we all make, especially when it comes to buying food. Food is an important part of our daily lives and therefore it is vital that we try to make the best choices.

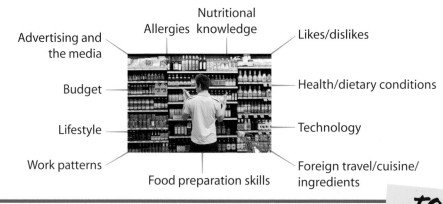

Nutritional knowledge
Allergies
Advertising and the media
Likes/dislikes
Budget
Health/dietary conditions
Lifestyle
Technology
Work patterns
Food preparation skills
Foreign travel/cuisine/ingredients

Budget

Income

Families on a lower income may be more likely to purchase cheap and convenience foods instead of fresh foods.

Expenditure

- If a person or family has more money to spend on food then they are more likely to purchase a wide variety of foods and try new foods.
- Many families choose to use lower-cost supermarkets such as Lidl to ensure that they can purchase cheaper products and get 'better value'.
- If money is available to purchase special offers and bulk buys then this is a good option for families as it can save money in the longer term.

Lifestyle

Health

- People who lead a healthy, active lifestyle are more likely to purchase food that is healthy and well balanced.
- People who do not lead a healthy lifestyle and do little exercise are more inclined to purchase snack foods, takeaway foods and convenience foods. Unfortunately

these foods are more likely to be high in salt, fat and sugar; therefore they will contribute to an unhealthy lifestyle.

Stress or anxiety

When stress affects a person's life this may alter the food choices they make. They may 'comfort' eat to make themselves feel better and reduce their anxiety levels. However, this may result in poor food choices.

Worldwide cuisine

Foreign travel

As travelling abroad for holidays is very popular, cooking and purchasing foreign foods is now very common. This has resulted in a wider choice of international ingredients being sold in supermarkets.

Cooking shows

Foreign recipes are regularly shown on television programmes. Consumers are more likely to purchase international ingredients after seeing how they can be used.

Nutritional knowledge and food preparation skills

Nutritional knowledge

If consumers are educated in healthy eating, a balanced diet and nutrients, then they will select foods that contribute towards a healthy balanced diet. If a consumer does not have even a basic knowledge of healthy eating and nutrition then they are unlikely to select fresh and healthy foods so convenience foods and foods high in fat, salt and sugar will feature highly in their diet.

Food skills

Practical cookery skills are beneficial for consumers who wish to choose fresh ingredients that require preparation and cooking. Many consumers lack basic food skills and as a result they will choose foods that require little or no preparation and cooking such as convenience foods, microwave meals and ready-made meals.

Quick Test

1. Explain three ways that consumers can save money when shopping for food.
2. Explain why foreign travel may influence food choice.
3. Why does stress affect food choice?
4. Explain how limited practical food skills may affect consumer food choice.

Factors affecting consumer food choice 2

Work patterns

Shift work

People who work shifts will find that their eating patterns are very different to those who work regular daytime hours. Shift working causes the body clock to become disrupted, and as a result they may select foods that are quick and easy to prepare such as microwave, ready-made meals, snacks or comfort foods high in fat, salt and sugar, which they feel may motivate them during long shifts.

Working families

- In many families the parents both go out to work and therefore there is less time to prepare food from scratch. As a result these families may purchase food that is quick and easy to prepare. Families may rely on frozen, ready-made and convenience foods that can be produced without much effort and time.

- Takeaway meals are common with families who have little time to prepare fresh meals. However they are not always healthy. In some cases takeaway meals can push you over the recommended daily amount of salt and fat, both of which can lead to a variety of health problems such as coronary heart disease, obesity and diabetes.

Retirement

During retirement income may be less than before and in some cases retirement may be due to ill health, therefore food choices may be restricted. Pensioners may select lower-cost foods and avoid more expensive ones such as meat and fruit. If an elderly person is suffering ill health then shopping and cooking may be difficult so they may rely on 'Meals on Wheels' or convenience foods.

Advertising and the media

TV

Television advertising is a powerful method of promoting food products to consumers. Advertising can be very persuasive and encourage people to purchase foods that they have not tried before.

Celebrities

Many food manufacturers use famous personalities to promote their product in the hope that this will encourage consumers to choose their brand. An example of this is the Walkers crisps advertisement starring Gary Lineker.

Technology

Online shopping

Since the development of the internet, food shopping has been revolutionised. Online shopping for food has many benefits, including convenience, wider choice and price comparisons.

Equipment

Kitchen technology has developed significantly and now consumers can purchase a range of equipment for food preparation. This encourages people to purchase new and varied ingredients that they would not have previously tried. Examples of technological developments within the kitchen include bread makers, health grills, combination microwaves, ice-cream makers, food processors and steamers and soup makers.

Health issues

Diet-related disorders

Consumers who are suffering from diet-related conditions such as diabetes, coronary heart disease, high cholesterol and coeliac disease may purchase specific foods to improve or control their condition. There are many food products on the market that are promoted as having health benefits, such as cholesterol-lowering spreads and yoghurts.

Vegetarians

Vegetarian food products are now much more widely available in supermarkets, and this has allowed vegetarians to vary their diet. Products that are suitable for vegetarians are clearly labelled to allow consumers to make an informed choice.

Continues over page

Likes and dislikes

Personal taste

Everyone has different likes and dislikes, especially when it comes to food choice. However, because of the large variety of food products available in supermarkets, consumers' likes and dislikes are catered for. Supermarkets are now larger than ever before. Therefore consumers are given a wide range of choice.

Peer pressure

Friends and peers may be a significant influence upon consumers when choosing food products. Children and teenagers are specifically vulnerable to giving in to peer pressure. Many feel pressured into purchasing foods that their friends are choosing, and unfortunately these are not always healthy options.

Quick Test

1. Identify four factors that may affect the choice of food purchased by a consumer.

2. Explain how a consumer may be influenced by peer pressure.

3. List and explain two ways in which the media may influence consumers' choice of food.

4. List four possible health-related issues which may affect the types of food purchased.

 Got it? ☐ ☐ ☐

Food miles

The term **food miles** means the distance that food travels from the production stage through to reaching the consumer; this is sometimes referred to as farm to fork. In some cases food miles are also calculated to include the disposal of food waste to landfill sites. The more food miles that a product covers, the greater impact it has on the environment and the more pollution it will contribute to.

Food miles: interesting facts

- In the UK, our food travels approximately 30 billion km per year. This involves food being transported by air, sea, road and rail.
- The transportation of UK food adds 19 million tonnes of carbon dioxide to the atmosphere each year. It is thought that two billion tonnes of this is caused by cars going to and from shops and supermarkets.
- Some 95% of fruit and 50% of vegetables eaten in the UK are imported.
- Locally sourced carrots travel 20 food miles, whereas conventionally sourced carrots accumulate 1838 miles!

Effect on consumer choice

The consumer can help to reduce the carbon footprint of a product by taking the following steps:

- check the origin of produce on a food label
- support local farmers and producers by using farmers' markets and farm shops and buy locally
- buy organic food stuffs where possible
- walk or cycle to the local shops instead of always taking the car
- investigate which foods are in season, and where it is possible to buy local seasonal produce
- bulk buy foods that are in season and freeze, store and preserve until a later date
- recycle food waste and packaging to reduce the amount being sent to landfill
- grow fruit and vegetables in your own garden or allotment.

Quick Test

1. Explain what is meant by the term 'food miles'.
2. Why is there concern about food miles?
3. Explain one way the consumer can help to reduce food miles.

Factory farming

What is factory farming?

Factory farming is a modern intensive farming method designed to produce large amounts of meat, poultry and dairy products as quickly and cheaply as possible. Many animals go through the factory farming method including pigs, chickens, egg hens, ducks, turkeys, sheep, dairy cows and beef cattle.

Factory farming is becoming more common in the UK and the rest of the world. As a result of this, some small independent farms are unable to compete and have been forced out of business or have had to expand into industrialised factory farms.

However, there is widespread concern about factory farming. Some campaigners have described it as 'the biggest single source of cruelty to animals' (see www.factoryfarming. co.uk).

Factory farming concerns and the impact on consumer choice

- **Ethical issues** – It is a cruel method of keeping animals for a variety of reasons; for more details see the information on individual animals opposite.

- **Environmental issues** – It produces real concerns for the environment. An example of this is the huge amount of animal waste that has to be disposed of.

- **Local area** – Communities may not be happy with a local factory farm as the large numbers of animals will create significant noise and smell.

- **Hygiene** – Some research has suggested that as the animals are kept in areas with high levels of excrement, this may increase the risk of bacteria entering the food chain, which is potentially dangerous to consumers.

- **Antibiotics** – As there are so many animals kept together in small areas, infection is common and farmers tend to treat all animals with antibiotics. The side effects on human health are uncertain.

- **Pesticides** – Factory farmers use high levels of pesticides on the animals to prevent disease and pest infestation. Pesticides may be harmful to human health.

- **Growth hormones** – Animals are forced to grow unnaturally quickly to ensure the farmers produce as much as possible; this is done through feeding the animals growth hormones. The effects on humans of consuming food containing these chemicals are very uncertain.

- **Small independent farmers** are pushed out of business by the large factory farmers who mass-produce food.

- **Taste and quality** of the products may not be as good as traditionally farmed items.

> **TOP TIP**
>
> In the exam be prepared to explain why consumers would buy free range eggs and organic produce.

Common factory-farmed animals

Pigs

Factory-farmed pigs are kept in very small concrete pens and are not given room to roam free. As a result, the pigs become aggressive and frustrated. Around 80% of UK farmed pigs have their tails cut off to prevent them biting the tails off other pigs.

Egg hens

Battery-farmed hens are often kept in very small, cramped and filthy conditions with up to five hens per wire cage. The hens are forced to produce as many eggs as possible, and this is done using artificial lighting and feeding. Some 80% of eggs are obtained by this method of farming.

Dairy cows

Dairy cows that go through the factory-farming process may have to endure both pregnancy and milking at the same time. They are overmilked daily and the calves are taken away after just a few days. As a result cows are likely to suffer from a number of serious conditions, including mastitis in the udders, foot and leg disorders and muscle wastage.

Chickens

Chicken sheds can contain as many as 50 000 chickens, causing distress amongst the animals as well as hygiene issues. The chickens are forced to grow unnaturally fast, and as a result their hearts cannot cope with the strain, and many die. Their legs may break under the strain of their unnatural weight. Ducks, turkeys and guinea fowl all endure similar conditions.

Quick Test

1. Describe what is meant by the term 'factory farming'.
2. List and explain four reasons why factory farming may not be beneficial.
3. Explain how dairy cows are factory farmed.
4. List two animals other than pigs, chickens, egg hens and dairy cows, that are commonly factory farmed.

Organic foods

What does organic mean?

Organic produce is now very popular in the UK. However it is a strictly regulated method of food production and is monitored very carefully from farm to production. Organic is a **sustainable farming** method that adheres to certain principles.

- No artificial fertilisers, chemicals and pesticides are used in organic farming.
- Crop rotation and adding compost and manure are used as a means of maintaining soil fertility.
- Animal welfare is extremely important in organic farming, and all animals are given **free-range** status.
- The use of drugs and antibiotics as part of routine farming is banned.
- Genetically modified crops and ingredients are banned.

The Soil Association

The Soil Association is a charity reliant on donations and on the support of its members and the public to carry out its work. In the UK. The Soil Association is one of the main organisations that certifies farms and food products with organic status.

The Soil Association symbol on a product reassures the consumer that the product has been approved as organic.

TOP TIP

Visit the Soil Association website for more details and interesting facts about organic food: www. soilassociation.org.uk.

Effects on consumer choice

Advantages of buying organic food	Disadvantages of buying organic food
• Some consumers believe that organic food may be nutritionally better. • As no chemicals and pesticides are used, organic food is thought to be better for health: for example, less likely to cause allergies. • Some consumers believe that organic food tastes better. • Consumers feel happier that they are supporting good animal welfare. • Consumers feel they are doing their part in protecting the environment. • Products are free from genetically modified ingredients. • As demand has increased for organic food, availability has increased through the use of local organic box delivery schemes. • As some products have become more in demand the price has been pushed down.	• Recent scientific research has claimed that there are very few, if any, nutritional benefits from consuming organic food. • The appearance of organic food is not as 'uniform' as traditionally farmed produce. • In some cases the shelf life of organic produce is shorter. • The cost of some organic produce is still higher than non-organic foods. • Not all organic products are widely available; therefore choice may be restricted.

TOP TIP

In the exam you may be asked to evaluate organic produce. Therefore ensure you can describe the advantages and disadvantages.

Quick Test

1. Explain what organic farming involves.
2. Name the association that monitors organic food.
3. Explain two benefits of consuming organic food.
4. Explain two possible disadvantages of buying organic food.

World hunger

World hunger refers to the millions of people who are currently facing the risk of insufficient amounts and/or poor quality of food. This is sometimes referred to as **food security**.

To simplify the above definition, world hunger is another term for **malnutrition**.

Facts

- Sources estimate that between 870 million and 1 billion people are undernourished in the world today.
- In developing countries a third of all deaths in children under five years of age are linked to undernutrition.
- A child dies from hunger-related causes every 8–12 seconds.

What are the causes of world hunger?

- natural disasters
- conflict and war
- poverty
- poor agricultural infrastructure
- crop pests
- overexploitation of the environment

Symptoms and conditions associated with malnutrition

TOP TIP

Malnutrition can also mean that a person is overeating. It does not simply refer to someone who is deficient in many nutrients.

Empty stomach   Diarrhoea   Respiratory infection

Depression/irritability

Infectious disease

MALNUTRITION

Impaired physical development

Impaired mental development

Micronutrient deficiencies   **DEATH**   Macronutrient deficiencies

vitamin A   anaemia   iodine

Food aid

> **Food aid** is a vital element of assisting the level of hunger/malnutrition in the world. Food aid can be described in various ways, but the most common definition is the **voluntary transfer of resources from one country to another**.
>
> The United Nations' World Food Programme (WFP) is the world's largest humanitarian agency that fights hunger world-wide.

Food aid programmes

Food aid can be given to developing countries in many ways. However the main programmes that are running through the WFP at the moment are listed below.

> **TOP TIP**
>
> **Vitamin A** deficiency is a leading cause of child blindness across developing countries. It affects 140 million preschool children in 118 countries. Deficiency in vitamin A can also increase the risk of dying from diarrhoea, measles and malaria.

Nutrition for under twos

By providing nutritious food and/or supplements for pregnant and breastfeeding mothers as well as the under twos the WFP aims to ensure that young children are given the opportunity to develop physically and mentally.

Food relief in emergencies

The WFP responds to man-made or natural disasters that cause an emergency food crisis. Here is an example of this type of aid:

'On 15 August 2012 the United Nations World Food Programme carried out the first in a series of airdrops to replenish rapidly diminishing food stocks for more than 100,000 people in South Sudan.'

Support to small farmers

The WFP supports small farmers in developing countries by educating and training them on developing more robust food production systems.

Meals in schools

Nutrition programmes in schools provide one meal or item per child. This allows children to concentrate on their lessons as well as escape hunger and poverty for a short period of time.

Food voucher schemes

Food vouchers are given out by the WFP to people who live in an area where food is available but they are unable to afford it. As well as supporting vulnerable families this also supports the local economy.

Food for training

The WFP Food for Training provides food rations for women in exchange for work that benefits their communities.

Quick Test

1. Explain the term 'world hunger'.
2. Explain two factors that may contribute to world hunger.
3. Explain how the World Food Programme can help developing countries.

Farmers' markets

What is a farmers' market?

At a farmers' market farmers, growers and producers from throughout the region sell their produce directly to the local community. The markets can be held either indoors or outdoors. The produce sold should have been grown, reared, caught or made/prepared by the producer, often within a certain distance of the market.

What's for sale?

At a local farmers' market there are many items for sale, and many producers on hand to sell their produce. At one London farmers' market it is thought that there are over 500 stallholders. As well as food, the stallholders sell household items such as flowers, plants, crafts and garden furniture. Here is a list of the most common types of food for sale:

- meat and meat products, including speciality meats such as venison and water buffalo, (in most cases the meat sold is organic)
- fish
- free-range eggs and duck eggs
- speciality cheeses
- seasonal fruit and vegetables
- honey
- herbs and spices
- organic juices
- alcohol, including beer and wine
- fresh bread
- speciality chocolate and confectionery such as tablet and fudge
- chutneys
- home-made pies.

Why are they so popular?

Over the last ten years farmers' markets have increased in popularity in the UK. They offer many benefits for consumers; however it is thought that one of the main reasons for their popularity is that the market provides a much more relaxed shopping experience.

> **TOP TIP**
>
> It is thought that in Scotland there are approximately fifty farmers' markets. Most towns and cities host these markets at least once a month. For more information and market calendars visit www. scottishfarmersmarkets.co.uk.

Benefits/factors that affect consumer choice of food

- Fresh produce
- Quality products
- Good value for money
- Reduces food miles
- **Farmers' markets**
- Healthier foods
- Sustains and creates local jobs
- Money goes back into local community
- Increases variety
- Seasonal foods available

Quick Test

1. Explain what a farmers' market is.
2. Give two reasons why some consumers prefer to shop at a farmers' market.
3. List four products that may be for sale at a farmers' market.
4. Explain how shopping at a farmers' market can reduce food miles.

Allotment gardening

An allotment is an area of land that is used to grow fruit, vegetables, herbs and plants.

The area of land is normally run through an allotment association. In most cases the allotment association leases the land from a public (local council) or private landowner.

The land is split up into small allotments, which are then leased to individual allotment tenants for an annual fee.

Over the last twenty years allotment gardening has seen a revival in this country. They are currently very popular amongst a wide range of people. The stereotypical view is that allotments are only for the retired. However nowadays many young people, including families, have their own allotments. There are many reasons for this, but generally people who have flats with no gardens or a house with only a small garden would be more inclined to want an allotment.

Why have an allotment?

- Cheap hobby
- Reduces food miles
- May increase vitamin D levels because of the exposure to sunlight
- Socialising and meeting new friends
- Relaxation and stress relief
- Encourages a healthy diet
- Home-grown produce
- Encourages gardening skills
- The food tastes better
- Helps the environment and the ecosystem
- Reduces pesticides on foods
- Encourages healthy lifestyle through physical exercise

What can be grown?

Most allotment gardeners will grow a combination of vegetables, fruit and herbs as well as plants and flowers. What is grown depends upon a number of factors, including the skill level of the gardener, the climate, the tools and facilities available and also the type of soil in the area.

Fruit	Vegetables	Herbs
Tomatoes, raspberries, strawberries, plums	Onions, potatoes, broccoli, beetroot	Parsley, sage, mint

TOP TIP

As allotment gardening produces fresh fruit and vegetables, this will encourage the owners to cook products from scratch, therefore developing practical food skills.

Seasonality

The easiest way to enjoy food at its best – and when it is full of flavour – is to buy and eat food that is in season. However there are also some other good reasons why seasonal food is such a good idea.

Why eat according to the seasons?

- Eating food that is in season reduces the energy needed to grow and transport the food.
- If food is in season then it is likely to be locally sourced and the price should be more reasonable.
- This supports the local economy and community.
- It allows us to reconnect with nature's cycle through the food we eat.
- Seasonal food is fresher and therefore tends to be full of flavour and taste.
- Nutrients may be higher due to the freshness of the food.

TOP TIP

Visit the BBC Good Food website and click on the 'seasonal' tab where you will find a calendar that maps out all of the food in season during each month.

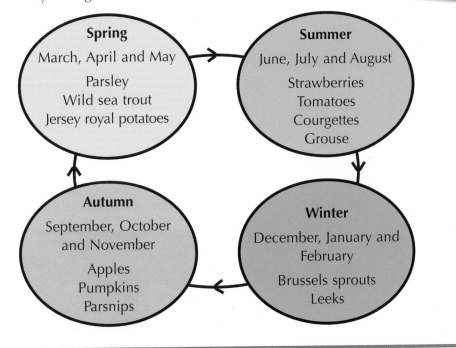

Spring
March, April and May
Parsley
Wild sea trout
Jersey royal potatoes

Summer
June, July and August
Strawberries
Tomatoes
Courgettes
Grouse

Autumn
September, October and November
Apples
Pumpkins
Parsnips

Winter
December, January and February
Brussels sprouts
Leeks

Quick Test

1. Explain why allotment gardening has become so popular.
2. List two factors that may influence what is grown in an allotment.
3. Give two reasons why it is beneficial to purchase foods that are in season.
4. With the help of an Internet search, list two foods that are known to be in season for each month of the year.

got it? ☐ ☐ ☑

Sustainability

The Earth's population is increasing so more and more pressure is being put on already-restricted energy, water and food resources. The concept of **sustainability** explores ways of providing these resources in a long-lasting manner that will have less impact upon the environment. Sustainability is an issue in everything from food production and transportation to disposal, and must be taken seriously by consumers, farmers, producers and manufacturers in order to ensure that we have the water, materials and resources to protect human health and our environment. The UK's Prince Charles said, 'I am urging the production of sustainable, local food as "vital" for the rural economy and communities.'

How can we encourage sustainability?

Consumers

- Use local, seasonally available ingredients.
- Purchase food from farming systems that are kinder to the environment, such as organic foods.
- Limit consumption of animal foods. Livestock farming contributes significantly to pollution.
- Do not consume foods that are known to be at risk, such as haddock and cod.
- Choose Fairtrade products.
- Avoid bottled water as this contributes to environmental damage through bottling and packaging. Simply use tap water.

The manufacturer or retailer

Most large manufacturers and retailers have policies about sustainable production: for example, ASDA's policy on protecting North Sea cod stocks. Asda only source fish from responsible regions and support the creation of a marine reserve to protect stocks. They also label their fish products to make sure consumers know where they come from.

got it? ☐ ☐ ☐

Food waste and recycling

Food waste

Reducing food waste in Scotland forms part of the government's campaign to develop a greener Scotland. The Scottish Government is committed to reduce Scotland's local and global environmental impact by moving towards a zero waste Scotland. To work towards this target the Government has a policy in place known as '**Reduce, Reuse, Recycle**'. Food waste contributes to pollution as waste breaks down in landfill sites and releases gases, which in turn play a part in climate change.

Here are some facts that may make you realise just how important it is that everyone works to reduce waste:

- In Scotland, almost one-fifth of the food and drink we buy ends up being thrown away – the equivalent of a family of four having another mouth to feed.
- Food thrown out whole or unopened costs the average household over £135 per year.
- Each year 389,000 tonnes of food and drink are wasted, costing the Scottish public £1 billion per year.
- Foods that are often wasted include fresh fruit and vegetables, drinks, and bakery items like bread.

Reducing food waste and factors affecting food choice
- Plan shopping and meals better and be more organised.
- Look carefully at portion sizes to avoid waste – do not overcook.
- Use a composter to dispose of unavoidable waste such as eggshells, coffee grounds and fruit peelings.
- Check with your local authority to find out if it offers a kerbside recycling service.

Recycling

- Energy can be saved when recycling compared to producing items from raw materials.
- Products get a 'second life' through recycling.
- Recycling is easy – points are located around cities, towns and villages as well as kerbside recycling.
- Recycling supports jobs though collection, processing and manufacturing.
- Valuable materials are put back into the manufacturing cycle.
- Pollution is reduced through less rubbish going to landfill sites.

What can be recycled?

Glass

Food and garden waste

Steel and aluminium

Paper and cardboard

Plastic including drinks bottles and packaging from food.

Quick Test

1. Explain what is meant by the term **sustainability**.
2. Describe three steps a consumer can take to contribute to sustainability issues.
3. Give two examples of how a product can be reused.
4. Give two practical examples of how a consumer can reduce food waste.
5. Explain three reasons why we are encouraged to recycle.

Fairtrade

What is Fairtrade?

Fairtrade is a system that allows farmers in developing countries to receive better, more consistent prices for produce. Fairtrade also ensures that farmers can secure local sustainability and working conditions for the farmers and their families are improved.

The Fairtrade mark is a registered certificated symbol for products that are sourced from producers in developing countries. It was first launched in the UK in 1994. To be registered by the Fairtrade Foundation a product must go through a certification process.

Benefits of Fairtrade

Fairtrade products benefit the farmer, the consumer and the environment.
Use the mind map below to assist you when revising the benefits in each group.

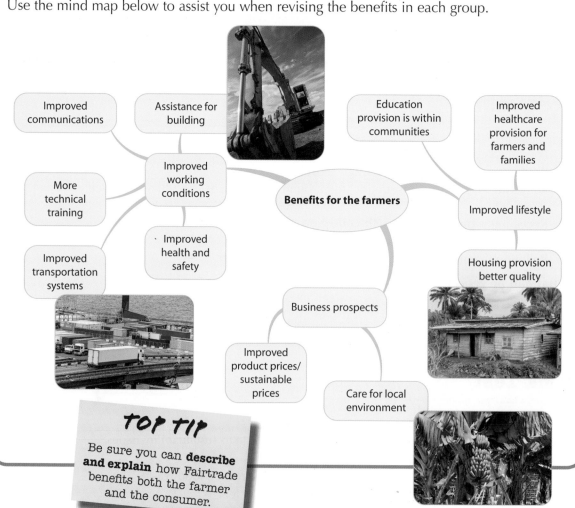

Improved communications

Assistance for building

Education provision is within communities

Improved healthcare provision for farmers and families

Improved working conditions

Benefits for the farmers

More technical training

Improved lifestyle

Improved health and safety

Improved transportation systems

Housing provision better quality

Business prospects

Improved product prices/ sustainable prices

Care for local environment

TOP TIP
Be sure you can **describe and explain** how Fairtrade benefits both the farmer and the consumer.

Factors that affect consumer choice

Fairtrade also has many benefits for the consumer, some of which are listed below.

- Fairtrade allows the consumer to make an ethical food choice.
- More products are now Fairtrade, so this increases consumer choice.
- Consumers feel they are helping to protect the environment.
- Prices are competitive with standard products.
- The products may be of a higher quality.

Common examples of Fairtrade food products are: cocoa, chocolate, tea, coffee, fresh fruit and vegetables, honey, herbs and spices, sugar, rice and pulses. There are also many other non-food Fairtrade products available, such as clothes, flowers and beauty products.

Fairtrade retailers

Many large retailers and independent shops stock Fairtrade products. However the Co-operative was the first retailer to promote Fairtrade, and first began selling Fairtrade coffee in 1994. Today, the Co-operative stocks approximately 260 Fairtrade products, giving them one of the largest ranges of Fairtrade products in the UK.

- More than 500 schools in the UK are registered as **Fairtrade Schools**. Schools can apply to become a Fairtrade school through the Fairtrade Foundation.
- Towns, cities and villages can all apply to become a **Fairtrade Town**. This status is awarded to an area that demonstrates commitment to Fairtrade principles and using Fairtrade products.
- Each year a **Fairtrade Fortnight** is held in the UK to bring focus and media attention to Fairtrade products and raise the profile of the issues surrounding farmers in developing countries.

Quick Test

1. Explain three benefits of Fairtrade farming.
2. List and explain three reasons why a consumer would prefer to select Fairtrade produce.
3. List four food ingredients or products that carry the Fairtrade logo.
4. What does the Fairtrade mark symbolise?

GOT IT? ☐ ☐ ☐

Genetic modification

What is genetic modification?

For centuries, farmers have developed new plant varieties by breeding plants with other varieties. However in **genetic modification (GM)** a plant's genetic material is altered by adding genes from other plants and animals. This means that the plant or animal has been artificially changed by science.

GM has caused a significant amount of concern amongst scientists and consumers and even after nearly twenty years of discussion the debate continues.

Factors affecting food choice

Benefits of GM	Disadvantages of GM
• Genetically modified plants can yield larger quantities of crops, bringing down the cost of food.	• There are serious concerns over the long-term health implications of GM foods.
• Plants and animals can be modified to improve characteristics such as quality, flavour and texture.	• GM foods will not be suitable for some religions and vegetarians as they may include genes from animals.
• Improved resistance to pests and droughts, which in turn ensures that they never spoil; therefore more food like rice is produced to prevent starvation in developing countries.	• Concern that the product is 'unnatural' and that nature has been tampered with.
• Nutrient value of the product can be altered: for example, more protein can be added to rice.	• It is thought that farming using genetically modified crops may cause environmental issues, e.g. cause some wildlife to become extinct.
• The shelf life of products can be increased, thereby preventing the consumer from having to shop as often.	• The welfare of animals may be at risk.
• Variety of products can be improved.	
• Products can be modified to suit demands: for example, leaner cuts of meat. As plants and animals may be less resistant to pests and diseases, then fewer crops will be wasted, which also keeps costs down.	

TOP TIP

• Many supermarkets do not stock produce that contains GM ingredients because of the unknown long-term health risks.
• Campaigners want a clearer labelling system, to allow consumers to make informed choices.

Quick Test

1. Explain what is meant by genetic modification.

2. Why are some people concerned about genetic modification?

3. Describe two benefits of genetic modification.

Food additives

A food additive is a natural or synthetic substance that is added to carry out a specific role in food products.

Food additives can be categorised by what they do when added to food.

Role the additive has in food products	Examples of food/s that the additive is used in
Colourings • **add colour** to foods, making food products look more attractive • **replace colour** that can be lost in processing	• sweets, icing, jam, jelly • canned peas or strawberries
Flavourings • **add or replace flavour** to foods, making food products taste better • **enhance flavour** of foods	• yoghurts, ice cream, sweets • ready meals, Chinese takeaway
Sweeteners • **add sweetness** to food products without having to use sugar	• diet drinks, jams, yoghurts, diluting juice
Preservatives • help **food last longer** by preventing bacteria multiplying • many preservatives are natural – vinegar, salt, sugar	• bacon, cooked meats, fruit juices, jam
Emulsifiers • help foods **mix** together that would normally separate	• mayonnaise, salad dressings
Antioxidants • help **food last longer** by stopping fatty foods going rancid • vitamin C (ascorbic acid) – a natural antioxidant that prevents fruit going brown	• margarine, butter • baby food
Others • raising agents – to raise and lighten baked goods • nutrients, such as vitamins and minerals, can be added to enrich foods	• cakes • breakfast cereals, margarine, flour

Continues over page

Food additives

All additives must be tested for safety before they are added to food. They are then given an E number to show they are safe. European legislation states that all food additives must be listed on food labels, stating their name or E number as well as the function they have in the food product. This ensures that consumers know exactly what additives are in their food products when deciding what to buy.

Why consumers would choose foods that contain additives

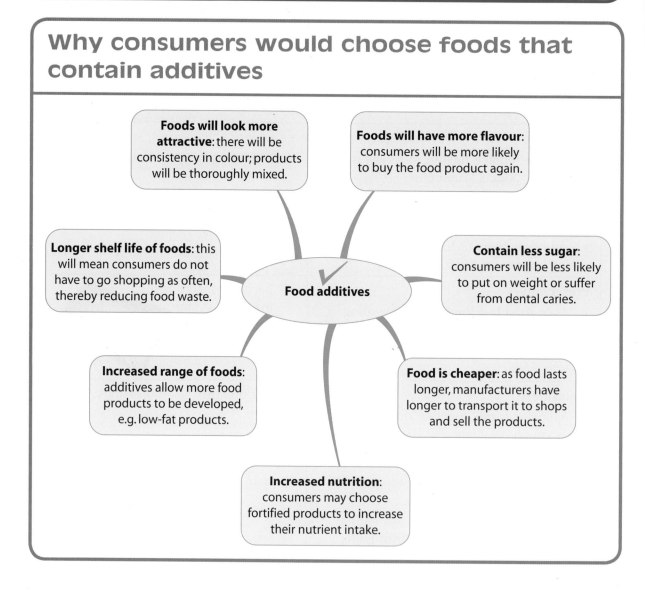

Foods will look more attractive: there will be consistency in colour; products will be thoroughly mixed.

Foods will have more flavour: consumers will be more likely to buy the food product again.

Longer shelf life of foods: this will mean consumers do not have to go shopping as often, thereby reducing food waste.

Food additives

Contain less sugar: consumers will be less likely to put on weight or suffer from dental caries.

Increased range of foods: additives allow more food products to be developed, e.g. low-fat products.

Food is cheaper: as food lasts longer, manufacturers have longer to transport it to shops and sell the products.

Increased nutrition: consumers may choose fortified products to increase their nutrient intake.

Why consumers might not choose foods that contain additives

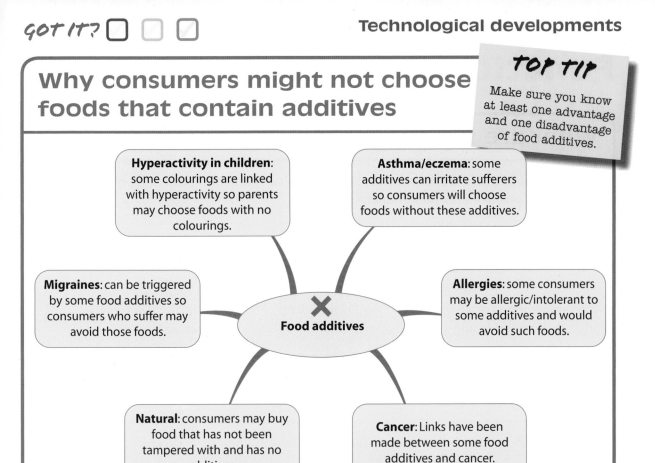

TOP TIP
Make sure you know at least one advantage and one disadvantage of food additives.

Hyperactivity in children: some colourings are linked with hyperactivity so parents may choose foods with no colourings.

Asthma/eczema: some additives can irritate sufferers so consumers will choose foods without these additives.

Migraines: can be triggered by some food additives so consumers who suffer may avoid those foods.

Allergies: some consumers may be allergic/intolerant to some additives and would avoid such foods.

Food additives

Natural: consumers may buy food that has not been tampered with and has no additives.

Cancer: Links have been made between some food additives and cancer.

Quick Test

1. State how a consumer would know if additives had been added to food products they were buying.
2. Why has the antioxidant ascorbic acid been added to apple baby food?
3. Name the category of additives parents may avoid because of hyperactivity in children.
4. Identify and explain two reasons consumers may **choose** foods that contain additives.
5. Identify and explain two reasons consumers may **avoid** foods that contain additives.

Functional foods

What are functional foods?

A functional food is a natural or processed food that has health-promoting benefits and may have a positive effect upon health.

Functional foods offer additional benefits over and above their basic nutritive value and it is thought that they may reduce the risk of certain diseases.

Supermarket shelves are now full of functional foods and the consumer has a wide variety of these products to choose from.

Functional foods are regulated by the European Food Safety Authority, which is investigating the health claims associated with all functional food products.

Probiotic foods

- Probiotics are foods that contain large numbers of different strains of live bacteria and other micro-organisms, such as yeast.
- Probiotics are often referred to as 'good bacteria' as they are associated with having a healthy digestive system and it is thought they may help to boost the immune system.
- However, probiotics have also been linked to improving other conditions, such as irritable bowel syndrome, constipation and diarrhoea.
- Probiotic yoghurts and yoghurt drinks are the most common type of probiotic product.
- From 1997 to 2000 the UK probiotic market grew from £3 million to £62 million.

Prebiotic foods

- Prebiotic foods contain carbohydrates that the body cannot break down naturally in the digestive system.
- Prebiotics assist the good bacteria already present in the gut by feeding them.
- They do occur naturally in certain foods, such as leeks, onions and asparagus. However many products that we can find on our supermarket shelves now contain prebiotics.
- There is continuing research into the benefits of prebiotics in the body. It is thought by some scientists that they strengthen the immune system as well as help to maintain a healthy digestive system.

Plant sterols and stanols

- Plant sterols and stanols occur naturally in small amounts in some foods, including grains, vegetables, fruit, nuts and seeds.
- They are clinically proven to reduce bad cholesterol (LDL) in the body and as a result this can help reduce the risk of heart disease.
- As they are so beneficial, manufacturers add them to popular food products. This process is known as **fortification**. Benecol and Flora pro.activ are examples of products produced with plant sterols and stanols.
- It is important to remember that products containing plant sterols and stanols are not suggested for use by young children and pregnant/breastfeeding women.

Omega-3-enriched foods

Omega-3s are polyunsaturated fats that have many health benefits. They can:
- reduce the risk of CHD and strokes
- improve concentration and learning
- ease the pain associated with some arthritis
- ensure that a baby's brain develops well during pregnancy and in the first few months of life.

Omega-3 occurs naturally in plant and animal sources. The main sources are green leafy vegetables, walnuts, rapeseed oil and oily fish such as salmon.

Food manufacturers add omega-3 fats to their products. Some cereal bars, yoghurts and yoghurt drinks are fortified with omega-3. Recently some varieties of eggs have been marketed as containing omega-3 fats.

TOP TIP

Cholesterol occurs in two forms: low-density lipoprotein (LDL) and high-density lipoprotein (HDL). LDL is bad cholesterol and HDL is good cholesterol.

Quick Test

1. Explain what a functional food is.
2. Give reasons why probiotic foods are thought to be beneficial to our health.
3. List two foods that naturally contain plant sterols and stanols.
4. Explain two health benefits of omega-3-enriched foods.

got it? ☐ ☐ ☐

Chilled and cook-chill products

Chilled products

Chilled products are foods that have to be stored below 5°C in a refrigerator. This slows down the rate at which any bacteria in the food can multiply, preventing **food poisoning** and **food spoilage**.

All chilled products have a **use-by date** so consumers know when to eat food by to ensure it is safe.

Extends the **shelf life** of foods.

Slows down growth of food poisoning bacteria, making food safer to eat.

Food is usually of a high quality.

Why consumers choose chilled products

Chilling does not affect quality, colour or flavour so foods are as each consumer expects.

There is an increased range of chilled products to choose from.

Allows them to buy a greater quantity of chilled products and store them at home.

TOP TIP

While chilling technology is very effective, bacteria are only slowed down so food will still go off eventually and can cause food poisoning.

What is cook-chill?

Cook-chill is a system of catering where the food is prepared and cooked in advance using normal cooking methods. However after normal preparation the food is then placed into containers and **blast-chilled** at 0–3°C. The blast chilling usually takes place within two hours of cooking. Cook-chill preparation of products normally takes place in large-scale food production.

Examples of cook-chill products

For consumers the name 'cook-chill products' conjures up ideas of supermarket ready-made meals. Although this is correct, cook-chill production is used widely and in more places than the supermarket: for example, in-flight meals, hospital and nursing home meals, hotels catering for large functions, some restaurants, fast food outlets, large corporate cafeterias and Meals on Wheels for the elderly.

Cook-chill production

As cook-chill production is so widespread, and there is such a wide variety of end-products, the production system will vary. However here is a standard example:

1. Select the raw ingredients.
2. Store the raw materials.
3. Prepare all the ingredients.
4. Cooking.
5. Portioning the product.
6. Blast-chilling.
7. Storage.
8. Distribution.
9. Reheating.
10. Service.

TOP TIP

Remember that for cook-chill to be effective food must be reheated thoroughly before it is served, otherwise it is likely that food poisoning will occur.

Effect on consumer choice of food

Benefits	Disadvantages
• Extends the shelf-life of products	• Certain bacteria may be able to grow
• Retains flavour	• Appearance may not be as good
• Reduces labour costs	• Some nutrients such as vitamin C may be lost
• Reduces food wastage	• Crisp textures cannot be retained with this technology
• Excellent time saver	
• May preserve nutrients	
• Increases menu flexibility	
• If used efficiently then improves food safety	

Quick Test

1. Explain why chilled products should be eaten by their use-by date.
2. Give reasons why the cook-chill food production system would be useful for a hotel catering for a large wedding.
3. Explain why it is so important that food is blast-chilled to 0–3°C.
4. Distribution of cook-chill products is a vital stage in the process. List the measures that must be in operation during distribution to ensure that the products are safe for consumption.
5. Give three ways in which the consumer benefits from cook-chill technology.

Modified atmosphere packaging

What is modified atmosphere packaging?

Modified atmosphere packaging (MAP) is a recent development in food packaging technology which has been designed to substitute the atmospheric air inside a package with a specialised protective gas mix.

The product is sealed in a package that contains natural gases in carefully controlled proportions. This way, oxidation is hindered, as is the growth of bacteria. Sophisticated machinery is used to flush out the air from the package and replace it with a different gas; the machine then seals the product.

Modified atmosphere packaging has many benefits for both the food producer and consumer. However there are also some disadvantages.

Effect on consumer choice of food

Benefits	Disadvantages
<ul><li>Increased shelf-life</li><li>Better quality of product</li><li>Reduces labour costs</li><li>Prevents wastage</li><li>Increases variety</li><li>Packaging is leak-proof and robust</li><li>Prevents cross-contamination</li><li>Prevents transfer of bad odours</li></ul>	<ul><li>Production costs can be higher, increasing selling price</li><li>Bulkier packaging so less eco-friendly</li><li>Strict refrigeration required</li><li>Certain bacteria may still be able to grow</li></ul>

Food products that use modified atmosphere packaging

- fresh meat
- fresh pasta
- processed meat
- ready meals
- cheese
- fresh poultry
- milk powder
- fish and seafood
- fresh vegetables

TOP TIP

Clostridium botulinum may still be able to grow in modified atmosphere packaging if it is not stored correctly. The bacteria will form a spore that can grow in the packaging and produce a toxin.

Quick Test

1. Explain the purpose of modified atmosphere packaging.
2. Describe how the growth of microbes is hindered.
3. List three benefits MAP would have for the food manufacturer.
4. Give three ways in which MAP would benefit the consumer.

UHT products

Ultra-high temperature or ultra-heat-treated (UHT) is a form of preservation that works by sterilising food products. This is done to kill bacteria and spores that can be harmful to consumers. UHT was invented in the 1960s and the first UHT products were available to consumers in the 1970s.

Foods that are processed using UHT are heat-treated to a temperature of 135–145°C. The food is only held at this temperature for a very short period of time: approximately 2–10 seconds. The product is then sealed into sterile containers.

UHT products

There are many products that undergo UHT before reaching the consumer, e.g. cream, yoghurt, soya milk, wine, fruit juices and some honey. However the most common UHT product is milk.

UHT milk

UHT milk is pasteurised and homogenised just like fresh milk, however it then goes through the extra UHT process. UHT milk is beneficial as it does not need to be refrigerated before it is opened. Therefore the consumer can store it at room temperature in a cupboard for approximately six months to one year. However, once opened, it must be treated as fresh milk.

> ### TOP TIP
> - **Pasteurisation** is the process that heats milk to 72°C for 15 seconds to kill bacteria.
> - **Homogenisation** is used to reduce the size of fat globules and disperse them more evenly in food such as milk. This creates a smoother, better texture.

Effect on consumer choice of food

Benefits	Disadvantages
- Extends the shelf-life of the product - Reduces food waste - Saves time shopping regularly - No refrigeration required - May be cheaper - Convenient and readily available	- UHT products may contain fewer vitamins (although this is debated and may not be the case) - The taste/flavour of some products may be altered - After opening, the products must be treated as if they are fresh: for example, opened UHT milk must be stored in the fridge

Quick Test

1. Which temperature range is used to carry out the UHT process?
2. How long does the UHT process take?
3. List and explain two benefits to the consumer of purchasing UHT products.

Organisations that protect the interests of consumers 1

Food Standards Agency

The Food Standards Agency (FSA) is an **independent** government department responsible for food safety and food hygiene across the UK. Within Scotland the FSA also improves food safety and protects the health of Scotland's population in relation to food.

Food Standards Agency
eatwell.gov.uk
Buidheann Inbhe-Bidhe

How it protects the interests of consumers

- Works with food manufacturers to help them produce safe food to sell to consumers.
- Develops policy on general food labelling, food standards and nutrition labelling
- Carries out research on food-related issues.

How it helps individual consumers

- **Does not** deal with **individual** consumer complaints but provides information through the following:
  - constantly updated information on the interactive **website**: for example, the hygiene ratings of local restaurants
  - production of **leaflets** on food poisoning, food additives, GM foods, labelling, nutrition
  - emailing consumers who register their interest to let them know of any recent developments, e.g. food that has been recalled.

Environmental Health Department

Each local authority will have an **Environmental Health Department** (EHD) that enforces food safety legislation.

How it protects the interests of consumers

- Environmental Health Officers (EHOs) **inspect** food premises to check they are working hygienically and following food safety legislation.
- If food premises do not meet food safety legislation, EHOs can serve an improvement notice or close the premises down.
- EHOs can provide advice and training for all food premises.

How it helps individual consumers

- If a consumer has contracted food poisoning or feels hygiene standards are not being met in a premises selling food, a complaint can be made about it to the EHD.
- Educates consumers by visiting schools and community organisations.

Trading Standards Department

Each local authority will have a **Trading Standards Department** (TSD), which will enforce fair trading and consumer protection legislation.

How it protects the interests of consumers

- Trading Standards officers inspect local businesses to:
  - test measuring equipment: for example, to ensure that consumers are paying the correct amount for 500g of apples
  - check pricing of food
  - check food labelling and the composition of food.

trading standards institute

How it helps individual consumers

- Consumers can make a complaint: for example, if they feel they have been misled by a local shop, or bought unsafe goods.
- Consumers can ask for advice.

TOP TIP

For each organisation make sure you can describe one main role that protects consumers.

Quick Test

1. Karen's son has just been diagnosed with hyperactivity caused by additives in food. Which organisation could she go to for more information about food additives?

2. Ben bought two boxes of cornflakes in the supermarket because a sign in the window advertised them as buy one, get one free. When he looked at his receipt he noticed he had been charged for both. Which organisation should he approach to make a complaint?

3. Erin bought her lunch in a local café. The worker who made her a sandwich had just handled money and not washed her hands. Later that day Erin had sickness and diarrhoea. Which organisation should she approach to make a complaint?

Organisations that protect the interests of consumers 2

Citizens Advice Bureau (CAB)

Citizens Advice Bureaux are **voluntary** organisations that offer free **independent** and impartial advice to consumers.

How they protect the interests of consumers
- CAB can provide information on a huge range of consumer issues including:
  - service or food in a restaurant
  - genetically modified food
  - weights and measures for buying food
  - faulty freezers, fridges, cookers, etc.
  - Citizens Advice Scotland, the umbrella body for CAB in Scotland, and Citizens Advice across England and Wales both deliver consumer education in the UK.

How CAB help individual consumers
- Consumers can visit a CAB in more than 250 service points across Scotland.
- CAB help consumers access information, fill out forms and write letters.
- The Citizens Advice Consumer service is a helpline which provides direct telephone advice on a wide variety of consumer issues.
- Adviceguide is the main public information website of Citizens Advice that provides consumers with access to CAB information on their rights; http://www.adviceguide.org.uk/scotland/

The Advertising Standards Authority (ASA)

The Advertising Standards Authority (ASA) **independently** regulates the adverts consumers see on television, the internet, in magazines and in emails and text messages.

How it protects the interests of consumers
- Develops advertising codes that advertisers have to follow to ensure adverts are legal, decent, honest and truthful. For example, food and drinks that are high in fat, salt or sugar cannot be advertised before, during or after a TV programme aimed at under sixteen-year-olds.
- The ASA is constantly checking adverts to make sure they do not break the rules. If they do, the advert will have to be amended or withdrawn.

> **TOP TIP**
>
> Think of any adverts you have seen recently for food. Have you bought the product? Did it live up to your expectations?

How it helps individual consumers
- Consumers can contact the ASA to complain about any advert they feel is not legal, decent, honest or truthful.

Which?

Which? is an **independent** organisation that campaigns to get a fair deal for all consumers. They publish the magazine *Which?*

How it protects the interests of consumers
- Carries out **product testing** to show consumers which products might be the best for them: for example, cookers, fridges, electric mixers. The results are published in *Which?*
- Researches consumer issues, including food, which it then publishes in *Which?* For example:
  - misleading special offers in supermarkets
  - traffic light food labels
  - budget vs. premium foods: can you taste the difference?

How it helps individual consumers
- Consumers can pay to become members of the **Consumers' Association**, and receive *Which?* magazine and access online information.
- Most local libraries have copies of *Which?* magazine, so all consumers can access the publication.

Quick Test

1. Which organisation could help each consumer in the following situations?

   (a) John wants to buy a new fridge that has plenty of space for his family's food and is energy efficient.

   (b) Helen has recently bought a new microwave and it is now not working. The shop she bought it from says it is not their problem.

   (c) Emma saw an advert in a magazine for a children's fruit drink. The advert stated that the drink would give children one of their daily portions of fruit, and showed lots of pictures of fresh fruit being poured into a glass. Emma bought the drink in a supermarket, only to discover that it was a powder and had to be mixed with water.

   (d) Lewis ate a meal in a restaurant chain but the food was cold when served. Although he complained to the manager at the time, he was not happy with the service and would like to write a letter of complaint to the head office.

2. Explain how the ASA protects consumers.

Statutory food labelling

Food labelling is extremely useful for the consumer. One of the main reasons for food labelling is to ensure that the consumer is not mislead and knows exactly what they are purchasing. However, there are lots of points of information on a food label that we read each time we purchase a food product. Some of these are **statutory** pieces of information, and some the manufacturers add **voluntarily**.

In the UK we have statutory bodies that are responsible for general food labelling. Food standards and nutrition labelling in Scotland is the responsibility of the Food Standards Agency (FSA). **Food Labelling Regulations 1996** is the piece of government legislation that controls food labelling.

Statutory labelling	
Information	**How does it help the consumer?**
Name of the food product and/or a clear description	• It tells consumers exactly what they are purchasing and ensures that they are not misled.
A list of ingredients (including food allergens)	• The label must contain a list of ingredients in descending order of weight. This ensures consumers can choose products to suit them: for example, by checking the sugar content. • Consumers can also read the label in order to avoid certain ingredients for allergens, and other health or ethical reasons. • The list must also state if any GM ingredients have been used.
The amount of an ingredient that is named or associated with the food	• This may appear in the list of ingredients. It is beneficial for consumers to clearly see how much of a specific ingredient is in the product. • For example, if they are purchasing fish fingers they can easily see what percentage of fish is in the product and are therefore not misled.
Weight or volume of the product 500g ℮	• Consumers use the weight of the product to compare different products and make decisions about the best value for money. • Food products may use the 'e' symbol which indicates that the weight of the product is the average weight.

An indication of the product's shelf-life: for example, the best before or use-by dates. The most common durability indicators on food labels are: • **Use by –** This is found on highly perishable foods and is an instruction for the consumer. It is likely the food will be harmful if eaten after this date. • **Best before –** It is usually safe to eat food after the best before date; however it may not taste as good. **Best before 26/06/2014**	• It is essential that consumers can easily see the durability indication on the label as this allows them to decide if they should purchase the product: for example, will they consume it before it reaches the use-by date? • This is also vital to ensure that consumers are clear about when it is safe to consume the food without incurring food poisoning.
Any special storage conditions or instructions for use and cooking **Once opened consume within 3 days. KEEP REFRIGERATED**	• This part of a food label gives the consumer the instructions necessary for safe storage, ensuring they can enjoy the product without increasing food poisoning. • It gives the consumer clear information about how to cook or prepare the product safely. • This information also allows consumers to make a decision if they have the time/equipment/skills to prepare the product.
The name and address of the manufacturer, packer or retailer	• This is very useful for consumers as it allows them to contact the manufacturer, packer or retailer with any comments, feedback or complaints they may have about the product.
The place of origin **Produced in the UK**	• Some consumers like to know which country the product is from on moral and ethical grounds. • Many consumers are also careful to select food products that have minimal food miles.

Quick Test

1. Explain what is meant by statutory labelling.
2. Explain why it is important for a consumer to be able to see the list of ingredients in a food product.
3. Describe what the 'e' symbol means on a food label.
4. Which agency controls food labelling in the UK?

Voluntary food labelling

Voluntary labelling	
Information	**How does it help the consumer?**
Recycling 	• Will help consumers recycle the packaging correctly and look after the environment. • Parts of the packaging may be recycled in different ways and this information is often given on a food label.
Nutrition labelling 	• Although nutrition labelling is voluntary for manufacturers, most products do have nutritional analysis on the label. This allows consumers to make a healthy choice when comparing products. • Nutritional labelling is a very complex issue and consumers may find it difficult to interpret the information given on a label. • In 2013 all major supermarkets and food producers moved to using a front-of-pack 'traffic light' system. This makes it much easier for consumers to make a healthy choice.
Barcode  8 686009 706568 >	• Barcodes allow the consumer to use self-service checkouts in supermarkets, as well as speeding up service at a conventional till, thereby saving time. • Barcodes also minimise the possibility of the consumer being charged the wrong price. • Barcodes allow the retailer to control stock more efficiently, thereby ensuring stock is available for the consumer.

TOP TIP

By mid-2013 the new traffic light system was in place. In the long term this should help to reduce obesity and coronary heart disease.

TOP TIP

Visit <u>www.greenerscotland.org</u> for more information on recycling and tips for recycling at home.

Recycling symbols

It is useful for consumers to know what symbols mean when they find them on packaging. Below are some of the symbols that can regularly be found on household packaging:

• This label from food packaging indicates that different parts of packaging can be recycled in various ways. The consumer must read each individual label to find out how to recycle the packaging.	
• This identifies the type of plastic.	
• This symbol is found on glass products and reminds consumers that the product can be recycled. Remember to sort glass into different colours.	
• The item can be placed in an aluminium recycling facility.	
• This logo means that the item contains wood from well-managed forests.	
• The 'Tidyman' symbol does not relate directly to recycling but reminds consumers to be responsible citizens and dispose of waste and packaging in the correct manner.	
• This symbol does not necessarily mean that the item can be recycled: However it means that the manufacturer has made a contribution to recycling in the production of the packaging.	

Quick Test

1. Explain the nutritional labelling information may benefit a consumer.

2. Explain how a barcode can benefit the consumer.

3. State two examples of food packaging that may have a recycling symbol.

4. How do recycling labels help consumers?

National 5 Health and Food Technology question paper

The National 5 Health and Food Technology question paper is worth **50%** of the total marks for this course. The rest of the marks come from the assignment that has been completed in school and sent to the SQA.

The question paper will be made up of **five questions**. Each question will be worth **ten marks** and the subquestions will link to a theme, such as organic food, health of an individual (pregnant woman, etc.).

The question paper will take the form of a booklet with space given for answers. It will last for one hour and thirty minutes. You should aim to complete each question in around **eighteen minutes** to make sure you answer everything.

The question paper will assess ability to integrate knowledge from all three units.

> **TOP TIP**
> Gaining as many marks in the question paper as possible will help you get an A or a B in this course.

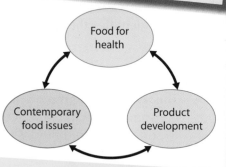

> **TOP TIP**
> There will be fewer questions from the Food Product Development unit as this has also been assessed in the assignment.

How to answer the question paper

- **Read** the question carefully, underline or highlight key words.
- **Read** any scenarios or information given carefully, highlighting or using symbols (see page 102).
- **Look** beside the question to find out how many marks will be awarded for a full answer. This way you can see how many points you are expected to give.
- **Give** the full number of facts/explanations/evaluations as short answers or a smaller number of points that you have developed further, showing your understanding of the question.

> **TOP TIP**
> Check you have answered your question and given as much detail as you can in your answer. Remember, you can get marks for developing points.

The next sections describe the five possible types of questions that will be found in the National 5 Health and Food Technology question paper.

State/give/name/identify

This type of question will allow you to demonstrate what you know by listing facts. Read the question carefully and make sure your answer links to the question.

Question: <u>State</u> practical ways a food manufacturer could reduce salt in food products. (2)

Answer: Adding herbs instead of salt in spaghetti bolognaise.

The answer above demonstrates knowledge of how to reduce salt and would be given one mark. You should now give an additional answer to get the second mark.

Describe

This type of question will allow you to define what is being asked in the question. More depth is required than a state/give/name/identify question. Read the question carefully and make sure your answer links to the question. Look at the mark allocation: if the question is for two marks you could make two accurate descriptions.

Question: <u>Describe</u> the role of the Citizens Advice Bureau (CAB) in relation to food for consumers. (2)

Answer: The Citizens Advice Bureau has a website that consumers could read for advice if they are unhappy with service in a restaurant. This advice could help the consumer write a letter of complaint to the restaurant.

This answer gives one description of what the CAB do and would be given one mark (Citizens Advice Bureau has a website that consumers can read for advice if they are unhappy with service in a restaurant). A second mark would be awarded as the answer has then been developed (This could help them write a letter of complaint to the restaurant). Alternatively, a second (undeveloped) description could have been given for the second mark.

Explain

This type of question will allow you to demonstrate what you know in more depth by making clear links with the question.

Question: <u>Explain</u> how advertising and budget could influence a teenager's choice of food. (2)

Answer: The teenager may buy a snack product they have seen advertised by a celebrity.

The answer above demonstrates knowledge of how advertising could influence a teenager and would be given one mark. You could now give an explanation of budget to gain the second mark.

Explain – continued

- This type of question will ask you to <u>identify</u> and <u>explain</u>. In these questions you should highlight key words in the question and use ✓ and ✗ symbols on the table to identify the most suitable recipe.

- For each explanation pick one piece of information from the table and link it to the words you have highlighted in the question.

- To get an extra mark try and develop your answer by explaining the point further.

Question: A supermarket has asked a local chef to cook a vegetarian recipe using a particular cheese for an in-store tasting session. (4)

<u>Identify</u> the most suitable recipe from the three shown below.

	Recipe A	Recipe B	Recipe C
Main ingredients	spaghetti ✓ mushrooms ✓ mince ✗ cheese ✓	macaroni ✓ cream ✓ peas ✓ cheese ✓	tagliatelle ✓ tomatoes ✓ peppers ✓ cheese ✓
Ease of preparation	***✗	****✓	***✗
Ease of serving	**✗	****✓	***✓
Flavour	**✗	***✓	**✗
Aesthetic appeal	****✓	****✓	***✗
Cost	££££✗	£££✗	££✓
			* low
			**** high

<u>Explain</u> why the recipe you have chosen is suitable for the scenario.

Answer: Recipe B is the most suitable. This recipe has the best flavour (taken from information in the table) for people to taste in the supermarket (link to highlighted word in question, taste) so this may encourage consumers to buy the cheese (explaining this point further).

The answer above identifies the correct recipe and is given one mark. The explanation shows understanding that a good flavour would be important for a tasting session and is given one mark. A third mark could be awarded for the explanation *why*. A further piece of information from the table should now be selected and explained for the fourth mark.

1. Information ➡ 2. Link to question ➡ 3. Explain why

Make adaptations to ...

This type of question will assess if you can look at a recipe or menu and use your knowledge to change it to meet current dietary advice or suit a situation. For example, you might be asked to adapt it for someone suffering from anaemia. You would then explain why you have made that change.

Question: <u>What</u> adaptations to this recipe could be made to help meet current dietary advice? (6)

Macaroni cheese

- butter
- plain flour
- whole milk
- salt
- macaroni pasta

Answer: The whole milk could be replaced with skimmed milk. This would meet current dietary advice to reduce consumption of fat.

This answer gives one adaptation that could be made to the recipe and would be given one mark (The whole milk could be replaced with skimmed milk). A second mark would be awarded as there is a link to the dietary advice (to reduce consumption of fat). Further adaptations should be made to gain further marks for this six-mark question.

Evaluate the suitability of ...

In this type of question you will be given a **scenario** and **information** and then you will be asked to evaluate the suitability. This type of question assesses whether you can apply the knowledge you have.

You have to show from your knowledge that you can make a judgement about whether or not the diet/meal/technological development/food issue is **suitable or not** for the situation.

Key things to remember:

1. **Read** the question carefully, <u>underline</u> or highlight key words. You must link to these in your answer.

2. Read all the pieces of information given, and decide if they make it **suitable** or **not suitable** for the scenario. Use ↑, ↓ On the table to work out if the person is eating more or less of each nutrient. Use ✓ and ✗ to identify if this is good for the person or not.

3. Choose **one** piece of information and then evaluate why this is **suitable or not,** linking clearly to the words <u>underlined</u> or highlighted in the scenario.

Question: A <u>sixteen-year-old girl</u> is a member of the <u>school hockey team</u>. She has been more <u>tired than normal</u> and wants to make sure she is eating the correct foods.

Exam technique

Taking account of the dietary reference values for teenage girls aged fifteen–eighteen, evaluate the suitability of her meals for one day. (6)

Dietary reference values for teenage girls aged 15–18					
Estimated average requirements	Reference nutrient intake				
Energy (MJ)	Protein (g)	Fibre (g)	Vitamin B1 (mg)	Vitamin C (mg)	Iron (g)
8·83	55·25	18	0·8	40	14·8

Dietary analysis of meals for one day					
Energy (MJ)	Protein (g)	Fibre (g)	Vitamin B1 (mg)	Vitamin C (mg)	Iron (g)
7·36 ↓✗	57·75 ↑✓	14·5 ↓✗	0·85 ↑✓	32 ↓✗	13·4 ↓✗

Information from case study

Explanation has been developed

Answer: The teenager is getting 7.36MJ of energy, which is less than she needs. This is not suitable as she plays hockey for the school team and this will contribute to her feeling tired.

Judgement

The answer above demonstrates understanding of the information in the table and your ability to link this to the scenario, plus making a judgement about the suitability for one mark (The teenager is getting 7·36MJ of energy, which is less than she needs. This is not suitable as she plays hockey for the school team). A second mark could be awarded as the evaluation has been developed (so will contribute to her feeling tired). Further nutrients from the table should now be selected and evaluated to gain further marks for this six-mark question.

Glossary

Adult – A fully developed and mature grown-up.

Advertising Standards Authority (ASA) – An independent organisation that regulates all adverts seen by consumers.

Aeration – To introduce air into foods.

Anaemia – A diet-related disease caused by insufficient iron in the body.

Antioxidants – Vitamins (ACE) that protect the body from damage by free radicals.

Baby – A newborn or recently born infant.

Balanced diet – When a person eats a variety of food and drinks that will provide them with the correct amount of nutrients their body needs.

Binding – To make a mixture stick together, normally using a liquid.

Caramelisation – Sugar is heated to a high temperature so that it changes colour and becomes caramel.

Children – A young human below the age of puberty.

Chilled products – Perishable foods that need to be stored at 0–4°C to keep them safe to eat.

Citizens Advice Bureau (CAB) – A voluntary organisation that offers free independent advice to consumers and is responsible for providing consumer education.

Coagulation – When heated, protein will turn from a liquid into a solid. This is coagulation.

Consumer – A person who buys, prepares, cooks or eats food.

Consumers' Association – An independent organisation that campaigns to get a fair deal for consumers.

Cook-chill products – Food is prepared and cooked by a food manufacturer then blast-chilled within two hours of cooking before being distributed.

Coronory heart disease – A diet-related disease caused by too much saturated fat, which can lead to a build-up of cholesterol, narrowing the arteries and thus making it more difficult to pump blood around the body.

Cross-contamination – The transfer of pathogenic bacteria from one food to another.

Crystallisation – Sugar and water are heated leaving a syrup. This is called crystallisation.

Current dietary advice – Healthy eating guidelines set by the government to try and combat diet-related diseases.

Danger zone – The temperatures where bacteria will multiply rapidly: 5–63°C.

Deficiencies – Lack or shortage of nutrients that the body needs.

Dental caries – Tooth decay caused by the bacteria in our mouths feeding on sugary food and drinks to form plaque.

Dextrinisation – Starch when heated will change to dextrin, turning the food brown, e.g. bread to toast.

Dietary reference values – The recommended nutritional intake for different groups of people.

'e' mark – EU symbol showing that the average weight system has been used.

Emerging markets – The ability of developing countries to contribute to the food industry.

Emulsifying – Enables foods to mix together that would normally separate, e.g. oil and water.

Environmental Health Department (EHD) – Department that will enforce food safety legislation within a local authority.

Factory farming – An intensive farming method that produces large amounts of meat, poultry and dairy products as quickly and cheaply as possible.

Glossary

Fairtrade – An organisation that allows farmers in developing countries to receive consistent prices for the food they produce.

Fermentation – Sugars are fermented by yeast, producing carbon dioxide, which can help bread to rise.

Food additives – Natural or synthetic substances added to foods.

Food aid – The voluntary transfer of resources from one country to another to tackle the level of hunger/malnutrition in the world.

Food allergy – An adverse reaction to eating specific foods.

Food manufacturer – The person or company that makes food products from ingredients to sell to consumers.

Food miles – The distance that food travels from the production stage through to reaching the consumer.

Food poisoning – An unpleasant illness caused by eating contaminated food.

Food product development – The process from generating ideas to the point when a new food product goes on sale to consumers.

Food Standards Agency (FSA) – An independent government department to improve food safety and protect the health of people living in Scotland.

Functional foods – A natural or processed food with health-promoting benefits.

Functional properties – The specific functions individual ingredients have that can be used to produce different food products.

Gelatinisation – Liquid and starch are heated together to thicken the liquid.

Genetically modified foods – Plant or animal genetic material that has been altered to change characteristics of the original food.

Glazing – To add shine to foods using milk, sugar or egg.

Haemoglobin – Found in red blood cells that carry oxygen around the body. Iron forms haemoglobin.

High blood pressure – A diet-related disease caused by high amounts of sodium that make the heart work harder to pump blood around the body.

High-risk foods – Foods normally high in protein or water that bacteria will multiply on. Often these foods are not cooked before eating.

Interrelationships – When nutrients work together in the body.

Lactation – When a mother produces milk for her baby.

Macronutrients – Nutrients that make up the main components of our diet and are needed in larger quantities.

Micronutrients – Nutrients that the body only needs small quantities of.

Modified atmosphere packaging – Food is packaged in sealed containers that have had the air within the packaging changed to contain less oxygen.

Nutrients – Chemicals found in food.

Obesity – A diet-related disease caused by eating more calories than the body uses in a day, which are stored as fat until needed.

Organic produce – Foods that have been produced without the use of artificial fertilisers, chemicals or pesticides.

Ostomalacia – Soft bones.

Osteoporosis – A diet-related disease caused by insufficient calcium, vitamin D and phosphorous in the diet. Bones become brittle and break easily.

Paired comparison test – Items of food or drink are compared for preference or for a characteristic, e.g. sweetness.

Pathogenic bacteria – Bacteria that cause food poisoning.

Profiling test – Items of food or drink are rated for more than one characteristic, e.g. sweetness, smoothness, spiciness, colour.

Ranking test – Items of food or drink are ranked in order of preference or by a characteristic, e.g. sweetness.

Rating test – Items of food or drink are rated on a scale (1–5) for preference, or for a certain characteristic, e.g. smoothness.

Seasonality – Taking account of what is in season (available naturally and locally) when purchasing food.

Sensory evaluation – Tests that find out what consumers think of the appearance, aroma, taste and texture and overall acceptability of food and drinks.

Shortening – Waterproofing of flour with fat to give a crumbly texture to foods, e.g. biscuits.

Spoilage bacteria – Bacteria that cause food to go off.

Statutory – Information that the law states must be provided for consumers.

Strokes – When high blood pressure causes blood to stop flowing to the brain.

Sustainability – Ways of ensuring that everything to do with food production has the least impact on the environment.

Teenager – A person between the ages of thirteen and nineteen; an adolescent.

Trading Standards Department (TSD) – Department that will enforce fair trading and consumer protection legislation within a local authority.

Type 2 diabetes – A diet-related disease caused by excess body weight, and thus the insulin produced in the body is no longer effective.

UHT – Ultra-high temperature or ultra-heat-treated. Foods are rapidly and briefly heated to 135°C–145°C to kill bacteria.

Unrefined – Non-processed, pure/natural form. Likely to be higher in dietary fibre e.g. unrefined sugar.

Voluntary – Information that may be useful to consumers but does not have to be provided by law.

Weaning – To introduce solid foods gradually into a baby's diet.

World hunger – The large number of people around the world who currently face the risk of insufficient amounts of and/or poor quality food.

Quick test answers

Food for Health

Page 9

Statement	Change needed to make the statement correct
Eating less fat will reduce the risk of tooth decay.	Fib. Eating less sugar will reduce the risk of tooth decay. Eating less fat will reduce the risk of coronary heart disease or obesity.
Eating less salt will reduce the risk of high blood pressure.	Fact.
Eating more fruit and vegetables will prevent colds and flu.	Fact.
Eating more oily fish will prevent Type 2 diabetes.	Fib. Eating more oily fish will prevent coronary heart disease. Eating less sugar will prevent Type 2 diabetes.

Page 11

1. HBV mainly comes from animals – contains all eight essential amino acids. LBV mainly comes from plant sources – lacks one or more essential amino acids.

2. HBV protein: meat, fish, eggs, milk. LBV protein: beans, lentils, nuts.

3. Polysaccharide.

4. Weight gain.

Page 13

1. It increases the LDL (bad) cholesterol and these fatty deposits clog the arteries, which can lead to heart disease.

2. Oily fish. It helps to reduce the risk of a blood clot forming, thus helping to prevent heart disease.

3.

Ingredient	Nutrient	Functions
Strong Flour	Carbohydrate	Supplies the body with energy
Olive oil	Unsaturated Fat	Concentrated source of heat and energy
Ham	Protein	For growth and repair of body tissues

Page 15

Statement	Change needed to make the statement correct
Water-soluble vitamins are stored in the body.	Fib. Water-soluble vitamins cannot be stored in the body.
Vitamin B1 releases energy from carbohydrate.	Fact
Vitamin C is an antioxidant vitamin.	Fact
Folic acid helps to form white blood cells.	Fib. Folic acid helps to form red blood cells.
Vitamins A, D, E are fat soluble.	Fact
Vitamin A is found in carrots.	Fact
You get vitamin D when you are exposed to the dark.	Fib. You get vitamin D when you are exposed to sunlight.
Vitamin D absorbs iron.	Fib. Vitamin C absorbs iron.

Page 17

Statement	Change needed to make the statement correct
Lack of iron in the body can cause anaemia.	Fact
Red meat is high in iron.	Fact
Calcium makes bones weak.	Fib. Calcium helps to give bones strength.
Calcium is found in milk, cheese and yoghurt.	Fact
Salt consists of sodium and phosphorous.	Fib. Salt consists of sodium and chloride.
Salt helps to maintain water balance in the body.	Fact

Page 19

1. Water helps regulate body temperature by sweating. Water is required for all body fluids.
2. Oats – act like a sponge to moderate blood sugar levels and remove cholesterol.
3. Whole grains – act like a broom to sweep out the digestive tract.
4. They work together to help prevent constipation and bowel diseases.

Page 21

Starter: Iron and vitamin C.

Main: ACE vitamins. Vitamin E improves the activity of vitamin A in the body. Once vitamin E has been used in the body, vitamin C helps to recycle it, therefore enhancing its action.

Dessert: Calcium, phosphorous, vitamin D. Vitamin D assists the absorption of calcium in the body. Without it the body cannot use the calcium in food. Calcium and phosphorous join together to create calcium phosphate, which helps to form and give strength to bones and teeth enamel.

Page 23

1. **Obesity**

Dietary cause: diet high in saturated fat.

Lifestyle cause: lack of exercise.

Heart disease

Dietary cause: diet high in saturated fat.

Lifestyle cause: lack of exercise.

2. A diet high in saturated fat can lead to a build-up of cholesterol which will gradually narrow the arteries, thereby causing heart disease. If a piece of cholesterol breaks away it can cause a blot clot to form. This blocks the artery as the heart is deprived of blood, causing a heart attack.

3. Diet high in ACE vitamins and total complex carbohydrates; reduce sugar intake; reduce fat intake; reduce portion size.

4.

Identify	Explain
Change the cookery method from frying the steak to grilling.	No additional fat will be added and this will allow the fat in the steak to drip away, thus reducing the amount of saturated fat consumed. This will help to prevent heart disease.
Swap the white baguette to a wholemeal variety.	This increases the consumption of NSP, which will help to remove waste and toxins from the body.
Swap the fizzy juice to water.	This will help to reduce sugar consumption, which could lead to weight gain and increase the risk of heart disease.

Page 25

1. Diet-related causes: diet high in salt/sodium; being overweight. Lifestyle-related causes: stress/insufficient exercise/high alcohol intake.
2. Feeling unwell, feeling tired, passing more urine, thirst.
3. Visit a dentist regularly/brush teeth regularly/limit sugary drinks and snacks.
4. Sugar in foods feeds bacteria in the mouth. Plaque is then formed, which causes tooth decay.

Quick test answers

1. People with low body weight; the elderly.
2. Have a diet high in calcium, phosphorous and vitamin D; reduce salt intake; increase amount of weight-bearing exercise; get enough exposure to sunlight; avoid smoking.
3. Julie has anaemia. This occurs when there is insufficient iron in the body. There are fewer red blood cells, which makes it difficult for oxygen to be transported around the body.

Page 31
Change 1: Swap white bread to wholemeal.

Dietary target met: Intake of wholemeal bread to increase by 45%.

Change 2: Swap haggis for vegetarian haggis.

Dietary target met: Decrease intake of saturated fat to no more than 11% of food energy.

3. Many manufacturers market a selection of ready-peeled and chopped fruit and vegetables to make it easier and to save the consumer time.

Page 33
1. Water-soluble vitamins, vitamin B/C.
2. Grilling – no fat is added and the fat drips away. Therefore the fat content is reduced. Stir-frying – very little oil is used and fewer nutrients are lost as it is a quick cooking method.
3. Steaming.
4. It contributes to a high fat intake and destroys nutrients.

Page 35
1. Breastfeeding.
2. First six weeks of their babies' lives.
3. **Breastfeeding**
   Advantage: Helps create a bond between mother and baby.
   Disadvantage: Father may feel left out.
   Bottle-feeding
   Advantage: Mother can return to work.
   Disadvantage: Cost of equipment.
4. Weaning.

5. Protein: to ensure body tissues grow and repair properly.
   Calcium, phosphorous, vitamin D: needed for bone and teeth development.
   Carbohydrate: needed for energy.
   Iron and vitamin C: needed to create red blood cells which transport oxygen around the body, thereby preventing tiredness.

Page 37
1. Iron and vitamin C.
2. Limiting intake of saturated fat will help to prevent obesity and heart disease. Limiting salt intake will help to prevent high blood pressure.
3. Anaemia
4. Advertising, peer pressure, dieting, family.

Page 39
1. Osteoporosis: calcium/phosphorous and vitamin D.
   Heart disease: reduce intake of saturated fat.

2.

Spina bifida can be caused by …	lack of folic acid in the diet.
An unborn born baby stores …	its mother's iron and uses it in the first four months of life.
Liver contains high levels of …	vitamin A, which is harmful to the developing foetus.

Page 41
1.

Abbreviation	Name	Definition
RNI	Reference nutrient intake	The amount of a nutrient that is sufficient for most individuals.
EAR	Estimated average requirement	The estimated average requirement for food energy or a nutrient.

Abbreviation	Name	Definition
LRNI	Lower reference nutrient intake	The amount of a nutrient that is sufficient for only a small number of individuals with low needs.

2. Safe intake.
3. Malnutrition.

Page 43

1. Occur within seconds of eating food. In extreme cases they can be life threatening.
2. Symptoms come on more slowly than with food allergies. Never life threatening.
3. Lactose and gluten.
4. Gluten-free diet.

Food Product Development

Page 45

1. Salmon – caught in the sea and then gutted.
   Chives – grown on a farm, washed.
   Bread – made from flour that is milled from wheat.

Page 47

1. Product testing, marketing plan, concept generation, first production run **Product** – packaging, **place** – where would you sell it, **price** – low/high, **promotion** – BOGOF etc.
2. (a) Product testing; (b) Marketing plan; (c) Concept generation; (d) First production run.
3. The marketing plan will include information on how the product will be packaged (product), where it will be sold (place), the cost of the product (price), whether the product will be part of a special offer (promotion).

Page 49

1. To find out the differences between similar products, to see if they could improve theirs.
2. Any point from the mind map.
3. Paired comparison test.
4. (a) Crunchy/crispy, (b) salty/crunchy, (c) thick/smooth, (d) colour/cold/smooth/fruity, (e) smooth/sweet/thick
5. Illness could alter a taster's senses, which would mean accurate results were not produced.

Page 51

1. Spoilage – causes food to go off. Pathogenic – causes food poisoning.
2. Vomiting, diarrhoea and abdominal pain.
3. Cross–contamination is when pathogenic bacteria from one food transfer to other foods.
4. As workers constantly touch food and can transfer bacteria.

Page 53

1. 5–63°C.
2. Bacteria will multiply quickly at this temperature and could cause food poisoning.
3. To prevent the temperature of the fridge rising into the danger zone.
4. (a) time/warmth, (b) moisture, (c) neutral pH, (d) time/warmth.

Page 55

1. (a) binding, (b) coagulation, (c) emulsifying, (d) aeration.
2. It will colour the scones.
3. Jam, sweets, fudge, tablet (any 2).
4. The cake will have a pale colour.

Page 57

1. Flavour and increased shelf-life.
2. Creaming or rubbing in.

Quick test answers

3. Pale, golden, black (burnt).

4. The fat coats the flour, preventing any liquid being absorbed, resulting in a crumbly texture.

5. Fat – aeration causing the cake to rise, flour – dextrinisation, causing the cake to turn brown.

Page 59

1. Used to add volume, bind, glaze.

2. Adds sweetness, aeration, caramelisation (to add colour).

3. Cheese – use less, flour – use less, milk – use more.

4. The chicken stock will change the flavour of the pasta sauce, and will make the sauce more salty.

Page 61

1. By increasing the sugar or liquid in a cake recipe.

2. (i) B, (ii) C, (iii) A.

3. Microwaving or steaming.

4. By increasing the sugar and fat.

Contemporary Food Issues

Page 63

1. Consumers can save money when food shopping by doing any of the following:
   - Visiting a low-cost supermarket as these have discount brands and are generally cheaper than other supermarkets.
   - Purchasing own-brand labels as these are cheaper than branded goods.
   - Shop when special offers are on, such as 'buy one get one free', as this will allow consumers to make savings and purchase in bulk.
   - Purchase foods in bulk that are in season and store until required, e.g. freeze or preserve.

2. Foreign travel encourages consumers to try new foods that they would not normally eat at home. Consumers will then come home and begin to make or purchase these foods.

3. Consumers who are under stress are more likely to purchase ready-made and convenience foods as they do not have the time or motivation to cook from scratch.

4. Consumers with limited practical food skills are restricted when selecting foods as they cannot purchase foods that require lots of preparation. As a result, they are more likely to buy ready-made, convenience food products.

Page 66

1. Any four from the following list: income, expenditure, health, stress/anxiety, foreign travel, cookery shows, education, food preparation skills, nutritional knowledge, advertising/media, lifestyle, work patterns, technology, likes/dislikes.

2. They may feel that if they are to be accepted by their peer group then they must choose the same foods.

3. Advertising – consumers may watch television adverts or read adverts in newspapers, magazines and on the Internet, which will then encourage them to purchase that product. Celebrities – seeing popular celebrities on adverts may then encourage consumers to buy that product. Price – some consumers will purchase foods that they have seen advertised with a special offer.

4. Coronary heart disease, high blood pressure, coeliac disease, diabetes, osteoporosis, constipation, diverticular disease (any 4).

Page 67

1. The distance that food travels from the production stage to the time when it reaches the consumer's plate.

2. Food miles are contributing to pollution because of the transportation costs of moving food around.

3. Checking the label to find out the origin of foods. Supporting local producers. Purchasing organic foods. Walking or cycling to the shops instead of driving. Buying seasonal produce. Purchasing seasonal foods in bulk. Reducing food waste where possible. Growing their own fruit and vegetables.

Page 69

1. Factory farming is an intensive method of farming that produces large amounts of products as quickly and cheaply as possible.

2. It is ethically wrong – people believe it is cruel to keep animals in small and unnatural environments. It can contribute to environmental issues because of the large amounts of waste generated. It can cause issues in the local area, e.g. noise and smell. Hygiene may be an issue with some factory-farmed animals, thereby increasing the risk of bacteria entering the food chain. Health issues – some factory-farmed animals are given large doses of antibiotics. The side effects of these antibiotics on humans are unknown. Health issues – high levels of pesticides are used in factory farming and these may be harmful to human health. Health issues – some animals are given growth hormones and the effect of these on human health is uncertain. It can push small local farmers out of business. The taste and quality of factory-farmed products may not be as good as traditionally farmed products.

3. By overmilking as well as enduring pregnancy at the same time. Their calves are taken away at a few days old to allow overmilking to continue. No grazing is allowed for the cows and they are often in poor conditions.

4. Ducks, turkeys, guinea fowl and beef cattle (any 2).

Page 71

1. Organic farming involves a farm using a more natural method of production. It does not involve artificial fertilisers, chemicals and pesticides but instead crop rotation is used as a means of maintaining soil fertility. Animal welfare is important in organic food production.

2. The Soil Association.

3. Maybe nutritionally better. Less likely to cause allergy due to no chemicals and pesticides. May taste better. Supports good animal welfare. Protects the environment. Free from GM ingredients (any 2).

4. Some research indicates very few nutritional benefits. Products are not as uniform. Shelf-life may be shorter. Cost may be higher. Not all products available in organic form (any 2).

Page 73

1. World hunger refers to the millions of people across the world who are facing the risk of little or no food on a regular basis.

2. The environment not being cared for. Crop pests. Poor agricultural infrastructure. Poverty. Conflict/war. Natural disasters (any 2).

3. Providing nutritious food and/or supplements for the under-twos and pregnant women, ensuring they can grow and develop well. Provide food relief in emergency situations such as natural disasters, in turn preventing starvation. Support small farmers by training and educating on better methods of farming. Providing school meals, thereby allowing children to make the best of their education. Providing food voucher schemes that enable poor families to purchase food. Training for women in basic life skills in return for food rations.

Page 75

1. A market where farmers, growers and producers from throughout a region sell their produce directly to the local community.

2. To support a local producer/community. Produce may be fresher. Fewer food miles. Better-quality products. Better value for money. Some products may be healthier. Better variety. Seasonal products available (any 2).

3. Fruit, vegetables, meat, fish, eggs, cakes/ pastries, bread, jam/chutneys/honey, cheese, herbs and spices, organic juices, some alcoholic beers and wine, speciality chocolate and confectionery, pies/tarts (any 4).

Quick test answers

4. The produce is usually grown, reared, caught and made in close proximity to the market.

Page 77

1. It allows people to grow produce, therefore is cheaper in the long run. Promotes healthy lifestyle. Encourages socialisation. Helps to reduce stress. Cheap hobby.

2. Climate. Skill of the gardener. The soil quality in the area. Tools and/or facilities available (any 2).

3. The food miles will be fewer. The foods will be fresher/nutrients may be higher. Supports local farmers. Quality may be better. May taste better (any 2).

4. Various answers.

Page 79

1. The process of providing resources such as energy, water and food in a way that will have minimal impact upon the environment.

2. Buying local foods. Buying seasonal foods. Purchasing organic foods. Limiting consumption of animal foods. Not regularly purchasing at-risk foods such as haddock and cod. Buying Fairtrade food. Using tap water.

3. Many ways, including charity shops, second-hand items, recycled into other products.

4. Looking at reducing portion sizes to prevent wastage of portions. Using a composter for peelings and some food waste. Planning shopping and menus to avoid unnecessary purchasing.

5. It will reduce global warming. Keeps our planet tidier. Supports jobs in the recycling industry. Energy can be saved. Fewer landfill sites in local areas.

Page 81

1. Allows farmers in developing countries to receive better prices. Ensures local sustainability. Better working conditions for farmers and their families. May be better for environment.

2. It is ethically better. It may help the environment. Product choice is improving. May be better quality. Prices are competitive (any 3).

3. Chocolate, cocoa, coffee, tea, sugar, juice, cereal, fresh fruit and vegetables, honey, herbs and spices, rice and pulses (any 4).

4. Symbolises that the product has been produced through the Fairtrade process.

Page 82

1. When plant or animal genetic material is altered by adding genes from other plants and animals.

2. There may be serious long-term health implications. Not suitable for some religions. Concern that the product is unnatural. May cause environmental issues. Welfare of animals may be at risk.

3. Larger yield of crop. Characteristics may be improved. Starvation may be prevented in developing countries. Nutrient value can be altered. Shelf-life can be increased. Variety can be improved. Leaner cuts of meat. Less waste. More economical (Any 2).

Page 85

1. All additives must be listed by name and category on food labels.

2. To prevent the apple turning brown.

3. Colourings.

4. Any point from the mind map.

5. Any point from the mind map.

Page 87

1. A food that has health-promoting benefits.

2. They contain 'good bacteria', which are associated with a healthy digestive system. They may boost the immune system. They may improve irritable bowel syndrome, constipation and diarrhoea.

3. Grains; vegetables; fruit, nuts and seeds (any 2).

4. They may reduce the risk of CHD and strokes. Improve concentration and learning. Ease the pain associated with some arthritis. Ensure a baby's brain develops well during pregnancy and in the first few months of life (any 2).

Page 89

1. They normally contain high-risk foods, therefore may contain food poisoning bacteria.

2. It means that the chef can prepare most of the meal in advance of the wedding and chill it until required for cooking.

3. To ensure the food is not in the danger zone.

4. Packaging is secure. Food is kept within the 1–3°C temperature range.

5. It extends the shelf-life. Retains flavour. Reduces labour costs. Reduces food waste. Saves time. May preserve nutrients. Better variety on menus (any 3).

Page 90

1. To protect the contents of a food package by altering the atmospheric air inside.

2. Oxidation inside the package is hindered.

3. Reduces waste. Reduces labour costs. Improves quality. Makes product look better. Prevents cross contamination. Reduces bad odours. Reduces risk of product leaking (any 3).

4. It allows greater variety of products. Reduces risk of contamination and food poisoning. Reduces bad odours in the fridge. Shelf life is increased. Better quality of product. Reduces waste. Reduces risk of product leaking (any 3).

Page 91

1. 135–145°C.

2. 2–10 seconds.

3. Longer shelf life. Reduces food waste so may save money. Saves time shopping for food regularly. No refrigeration required. May be cheaper than fresh. Convenient (any 2).

Page 93

1. Food Standards Agency website.

2. Trading Standards Department.

3. Environmental Health Department.

Page 95

1. (a) Consumers' Association, (b) Citizens Advice Bureau, (c) Advertising Standards Authority, (d) Citizens Advice Bureau.

2. ASA has advertising codes in place so that consumers are not misled.

Page 97

1. Pieces of information that the manufacturer must put on a food label.

2. They may have a food allergy or intolerance or they may wish to avoid certain ingredients for religious or cultural reasons.

3. The average weight of the product.

4. The Food Standards Agency.

Page 99

1. By providing detailed information that allows consumers to make informed choices.

2. Allows them to use self-service checkouts, which saves time. Reduces the risk of consumers being charged the wrong price. More efficient stock system, ensuring better stock availability.

3. Plastic/glass/aluminium.

4. They help consumers recycle packaging correctly. Parts of the packaging may be recycled in different ways and this information is often provided on food labels.